A SURVEY OF

World Cultures

AFRICA

Ken Levine

AGS®
American Guidance Service, Inc.
Circle Pines, MN 55014-1796

THE AUTHOR

Ken Levine has published numerous non-fiction articles before writing this book. In addition, he teaches on the secondary level in Baltimore County, Maryland.

PHOTO ACKNOWLEDGMENTS

Cover Photograph: Greater Grace Missions Department
Chapter 1: open, Mark Morin; p. 3 (top), James Kennedy, (bottom) from *Europus Kolonien*; p. 7, James Kennedy; p. 13, courtesy of National Geographic; p. 15, Library of Congress
Chapter 2: open, UN photo/E. Darroch; p. 30, Library of Congress
Chapter 3: open, James Kennedy
Chapter 4: open, Library of Congress; pp. 51 52, 55, 57, United Nations; p. 59, Food and Agriculture Organization (F. Mattoili); p. 61, Library of Congress
Chapter 5: open, AFP photo; p. 70 (top and bottom), AFP photo; p. 71, AFP photo; p. 72, United Nations; p. 73, AP Wirephoto; p. 77 (top) United Nations/Aid/Purcell, (bottom) United Nations; p. 81, Library of Congress; p. 84, United Nations
Chapter 6: open, The Image Bank; p. 91, Library of Congress; p. 92, Library of Congress; p. 94, from *The Last Journals of David Livingstone;* p. 98, from *The Illustrated London News* supplement; p. 103, United Nations photo/AID/Purcell; p. 111, Library of Congress
Chapter 7: open, United Nations/Y. Nagata; p. 119, Marcel Lewinski; p. 121, Donald C. Holsinger; pp. 122, 123, 124, 125, 126, Library of Congress

EDITORIAL ADVISORY BOARD

STAFF

Vice President of Product Development:	Barbara Kondrchek
Editors:	T. Sandra Fleming
	Donna Babylon
	Mary D. Szark
Typesetting:	Lynna Bright
Design and Layout:	Gary King
Artwork:	Carol Munschauer
Cover Design:	Norm Myers

ISBN: 0-88671-671-3
Order Number: 80332
(Previously ISBN: 0-7916-0008-4)

A 0 9 8 7 6

CONTENTS

Chapter 3: Equatorial West Africa

Chapter 4: South Sahara Africa

Chapter 5: Southern Africa

Chapter 6: Eastern Africa

Chapter 7: North Africa

Glossary

Index

INTRODUCTION

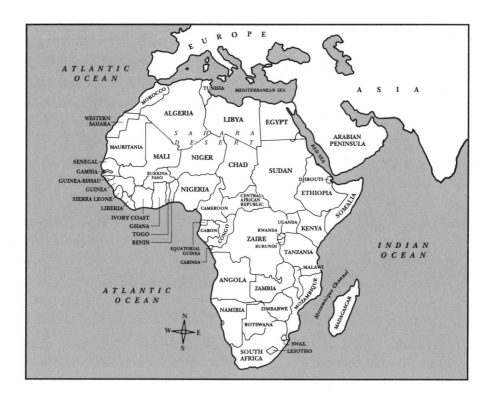

T oday, we are in the position of knowing quite a lot about Africa— and, at the same time, not knowing enough. Our newspapers are full of the daily events that occur on the *continent* of Africa. What we sometimes lack is the overall picture into which each of these news events may be fitted.

This book is designed to give you a full picture of modern Africa.

Africa is the second largest continent in the world. All of the land of the United States could fit within its borders. Africa is bordered on the west by the Atlantic Ocean and on the east by the Indian Ocean. To the north and the northeast are the Mediterranean Sea, the Suez Canal, and the Red Sea. The Cape of Good Hope lies at this continent's southernmost tip.

In Africa can be found steaming rain forests, dry deserts, mountain peaks, endless grasslands, and miles of beautiful coastline. The human population and *culture* are as varied as the geography. In fact, in Africa there are over 2,000 different ethnic groups and over 800 languages spoken!

What is culture? Humans are believed to have lived on the Earth for a very long period of time. During this time, the way in which people live has changed. Humans have learned to adapt and use their enviornment to survive. The climate and the kinds of food that were available gave people certain choices. They figured out what to use for clothing and shelter to keep themselves warm and dry and what to eat to make themselves strong and healthy. Most importantly, humans have learned to communicate. This procss of adapting to the environment and learning how to communicate marked the beginning of culture. Before language, culture could only develop so far. People needed language to share their knowledge with each other.

Some people think that culure is something fancy. They say that fine art and opera are cultural things. Although fine art and opera are part of culture, they are not the only parts.

The people who study culture are called social scientists. These scientists say that culture involves every part of life. In a way, culture is life. It is the way of life followed by a group of people. It includes art and music. More importantly, it includes beliefs, customs, inventions, languages, technology, and traditions that are shared by a group of people.

In this book, you will be looking at the cultural patterns developed by the peoples of Africa. You will be introduced to the *geography* of the various regions of Africa and see how this setting has affected the history, *economics,* and culture of the African peoples. The text explores some of the successes, problems, and prospects for the future of the developing nations of Africa.

Remember that the real story of Africa is its people, just as the story of the United States or of any other nation is primarily a story of its people.

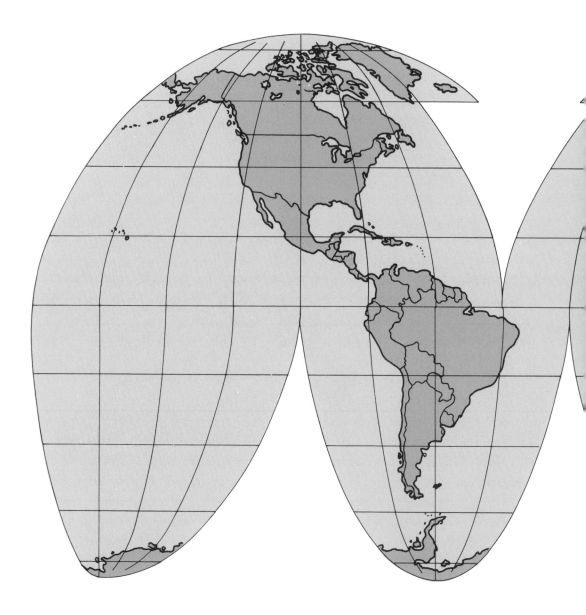

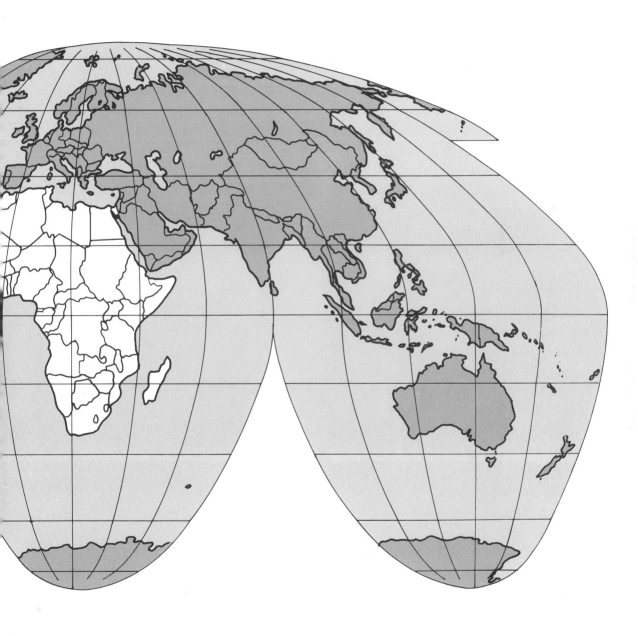

AFRICA

COASTAL WEST AFRICA

F A C T S	• A popular form of recreation in Liberia is going to the YMCA. • European culture has affected the traditional beliefs of West Africa. • The basic unit of money in Senegal is the franc. • The President of Guinea serves a seven-year term. • Independence Day in Gambia is celebrated on February 18.

PART 1:
Atlantic Coast Countries

West Africa is one of the most densely settled parts of Africa. The people have settled mainly on the *coastal plain* and on the dry *savanna* region along the southern edge of the Sahara Desert. This area is called the *Sahel.*

Today, there are more than 500 African ethnic groups living in West Africa. *Bantu*-speaking peoples make up the largest *ethnic groups.* They live in the forest regions near the coast.

These coastal peoples were the first to come into contact with the Europeans. They were also the first to suffer from the effects of the slave trade. Christianity was introduced to the coastal peoples by European missionaries.

The peoples of the much drier Sahel region have had a long history of trade and contact with the Islamic civilization across the Sahara Desert in North Africa.

COASTAL WEST AFRICA

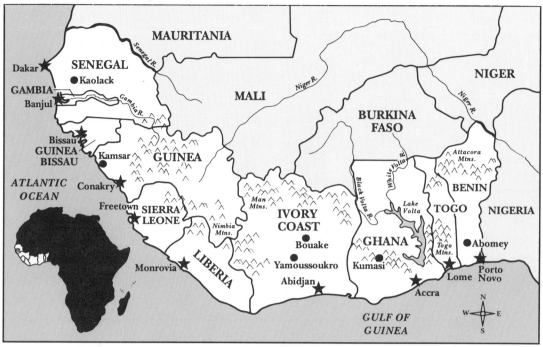

Map Study: *What is the largest country in Coastal West Africa? What two rivers feed Lake Volta in Ghana? In what two countries do you find the Togo Mountains? Near what two bodies of water do you find the capital cities of each country? Which capital city is located farthest north?*

Despite extreme cultural pressure from *Islam* and *Christianity*, many traditional beliefs in nature and in spiritual beings have continued. Both Islamic and Christian ideas have been adapted to the traditional West African culture.

Coastal West Africa consists of eleven different countries. These countries can be divided into two different regions: the Atlantic Coast countries and the Guinea Coast countries.

Senegal and Gambia

Senegal (sen i GAWL) is located at the western extreme of Coastal West Africa. Almost all of the land of Senegal lies in Sahel, a flat dry savanna or grassland. Senegal surrounds the nation of Gambia (GAM bee uh). This unusual situation exists because, in the past, Senegal was a French colony and Gambia was a British colony.

The people of Senegal and Gambia consist of mainly five ethnic

Men and women work in factories that produce furniture, canned goods, shoes, and household utensils.

guage of Senegal, but local traditional languages are also very important.

Most of the people of Senegal and Gambia make a living through farming on the savanna. Peanuts *(groundnuts)*, often grown in *irrigated* fields are the main *cash crop* for *export*. Corn, rice, *millet,* and *sorghum* are also grown. In addition to these crops, farmers raise cattle, chickens, sheep, and goats. Gambians depend on the Gambia River as a water supply for farming.

Senegal has the least developed economy of the Atlantic Coast countries. Dakar has factories that pro-

groups. The largest, called the Wulaf or Wolof, make up about one-third of the population. The other ethnic groups include the Fulani, the Serer, the Tukolor, and the Mandingo. Islam is the religion of most of the people.

Traditional culture is still strong. The peoples of the region have adapted much from the outside. Gambians speak English as well as their traditional languages. Senegal was the center of the French empire in West Africa. Dakar (DAK ahr), its capital, was the main city of the region. French is the official lan-

The Wolofs are one of the major ethnic groups that live in Senegal.

cess cotton, rice, and phosphate ore. Construction, electronics, and government services are important activities that create jobs.

Many women of Senegal have become active in the work force. A number of women are successful owners and managers of retail businesses. Some women have moved into other professions, particularly nursing and teaching but also medicine and law.

Since the prosperity of the two countries depends on one crop (monoculture), the nation's economy rises and falls with the price of peanuts.

History of Senegal and Gambia

Senegal and Gambia have a long and colorful history. That history is told orally by a *griot*, a traditional historian who recites poems telling of the deeds of the past. The griots have formed a long unbroken chain of history in an area of the world where history books were written only in Arabic. Traditional customs and beliefs are passed down from generation to generation in the form of stories. Being a griot in Senegal is much like being a history teacher or a historian in the United States.

The Gambia River has always played a major role in the history of the Gambia, as it is sometimes called. Beginning in the 1600s, slaves were traded along its banks. One village on the banks of this river is the city of Juffure. Writer Alex Haley traced his ancestors to this city and wrote the story of the origin of his own Mandingo family. Perhaps you have seen the movie *Roots*, which is based on Haley's book of the same name.

R
E
V
I
E
W

Directions:
Write *True* or *False* for each statement.
1. Most farming in Senegal is done on the savanna.
2. Peanuts are exported by both Senegal and Gambia.
3. In addition to traditional languages, English is spoken in Gambia and French in Senegal.
4. Dakar is a city through which most travelers must pass to visit Gambia.
5. The griots of Senegal are much like history teachers in America.
6. Alex Haley, in his novel *Roots*, traced his ancestors to a region of Sierra Leone.

PART 2:
Guinea and Guinea-Bissau

Southeast of Senegal and Gambia is the *Republic* of Guinea (GIN ee). Its *topography* is that of a plain broken by rolling hills. This *plain* is covered by tall tree savannas and dry forests. Guinea has both *fertile* farmland and valuable mineral resources. Cash crops include coffee, bananas, peanuts, and palm products from oil palm trees. This oil is used to make cosmetics, soap, and cooking oils. Palm kernels are used to make food and starch, while the palm fiber is used to make mats and rope. *Cassava*, a local plant that has an edible root, is the main food crop raised. Rice, corn, bananas, and pineapples are also raised for food.

Guinea produces one-third of the world's *bauxite*, a valuable mineral ore used to make aluminum. In addition, Guinea has large deposits of iron ore as well as gold and diamond mines.

Guinea has a proud historical tradition. During the 700s, Guinea was a major trading kingdom called Ghinea. Later, the country became a possession of France. After long years as a French colony, the people of Guinea voted in 1958 to become independent under the leadership of Sekou Touré.

Three major ethnic groups live in Guinea. The largest is the Fulani. Next in size are the Mandingo and the Susu. Within the forests of Guinea also live the Kissi, the Guerze, and the Loma. Most of the people of Guinea, regardless of their particular ethnic background, live in small villages. Most of the Fulani and the Mandingo are *Muslims*. The Susu and the smaller ethnic groups follow local religions. The official language of the country is French.

Cassava is a small shrub-like plant grown in Guinea. Its roots are used to make tapioca.

Guinea-Bissau: A Tropical Land

Guinea-Bissau (gin ee bis AUU) used to be known as Portuguese Guinea. It is one of the smallest countries in Africa. The capital city of Guinea-Bissau is Bissau (bis AUU). It is the only city of any significant size in this tiny country. The city was an important port during the Portuguese slave trade. The official language of the country is Portuguese.

This country's land is flat and has many rivers. Guinea-Bissau's climate is typical of a *tropical* country. It has a dry season during which there is little or no rain. This season lasts from December to May. The rainy season lasts from June to November, with the heaviest rains coming in July and August.

Living Conditions

Ninety percent of the people in Guinea-Bissau earn their living from farming. Many different kinds of crops are grown. Farmers grow rice, cassava, palm kernels, maize, peanuts, coconuts, and cotton. The farmers of Guinea-Bissau are mainly *subsistence* farmers. That term means that they usually grow food only for their own families rather than for sale. However, peanuts and palm oil are export crops.

Most of the people of Guinea-Bissau live in small villages throughout the country. The houses are very similar to those in neighboring countries—usually made of mud and straw with a thatched roof.

Many different ethnic groups can be found in Guinea-Bissau. The largest of these groups are the Balante, the Fulani, the Manjako, and the Mandingo (sometimes called Malinke). There are perhaps twenty other ethnic groups living in Guinea-Bissau.

R E V I E W

Directions:
Answer the questions in complete sentences.
1. What is the capital city of Guinea-Bissau?
2. What two products make the land in Guinea valuable?
3. What Guinean crop has an edible root?
4. Why do you think that Guinea-Bissau was once known as Portuguese Guinea?
5. Which ethnic groups living in Guinea can also be found in Gambia, Senegal, or Guinea-Bissau?

PART 3:
Sierra Leone and Liberia

Continuing south along the coast of West Africa, we come to Sierra Leone (see er uh lee OHN). A very large portion of the population here are farmers. Most of Sierra Leone's farmers grow rice and cassava as their main food crops. Some farmers also grow a type of palm tree that produces *piassava*. Piassava is exported and used to make brooms and brushes. Other cash (export) crops are coffee and *cacao,* which is used in making chocolate.

Textile Dyeing and Other Industries

A traditional art, *textile* dyeing, has developed into an important industry in Sierra Leone. Originally, dyes made from vegetables were used. Today, commercial dyes are used to produce the finished goods.

Women dominate the textile dyeing industry. Many times a successful dyer will employ other women or family members to produce the colorful cloth. Textile dyers earn a good income and are considered to be fashion leaders.

Other industries are centered around food processing and building supplies.

Diamonds Are an Important Export

The people of Sierra Leone have one other product to export—diamonds. These stones are mined from gravel beds as little as four feet deep. Many of the diamonds are used for industrial purposes. However, many stones are also cut and polished and sold as gems. These diamonds bring a great deal of money to the farmers of Sierra Leone.

Living in Sierra Leone

The country of Sierra Leone has many villages but few large cities. Its capital city is Freetown. This city has

High-rise apartment buildings are commonly found in cities in Sierra Leone.

many modern buildings and a large open air market. In contrast, houses in villages are usually made from mud and have thatched roofs.

The Peoples of Sierra Leone

The people of Sierra Leone come chiefly from two ethnic groups. The Mende live in the south of the country, and the Temne live in the north. Many descendants of mixed races also live throughout the country. These people are called Krios, or *Creoles,* in English. Their ancestors came mostly from freed slaves and whites from England and Canada. The official language of Sierra Leone is English.

Liberia

Liberia (ly BIR ee uh) is located on the bulge of West Africa. It is bounded by Sierra Leone, Guinea, and the Ivory Coast. Its coastal plain touches both the Atlantic Ocean and the *Gulf* of Guinea.

Liberia is divided into three zones. Along the coast are *mangrove* swamps. Most of the inland area is plains covered with tall tree savannas and tropical *rain forests.* Farther inland is an area of low mountains covered with thick, wet tropical forests. The country is divided by 15 rivers, some of which are navigable.

Most Liberians practice *subsistence* farming. Cassava and rice are the main food crops. Coffee, cacao, piassava, and palm products are the main export crops. Rubber plantations owned by the American Firestone Rubber Company once controlled the Liberian economy. However, the development of synthetic rubber has reduced the importance of this product.

Today, the mining of large deposits of high grade iron ore has helped the economy of Liberia. *Bauxite,* used to make aluminum, is mined both in Liberia and Sierra Leone. So is *rutile* (ROO teel) titanium ore, a strong lightweight metal used in the manufacture of jet planes and spacecrafts.

Settlements for Freed Slaves

It is of interest to note that both Liberia and Sierra Leone were founded as settlements for freed slaves. Liberia was founded in 1822 by black freedmen from the United States. The name Liberia comes from the Latin word "liber" which means "free." About 5 percent of the 2.4 million Liberians can trace their descent from freed slaves.

The country became a republic in 1847 with a constitution and government modeled after those of the

United States. The Liberians speak English, practice Christianity, and follow Western styles of social organization.

Beginning in 1787, the British Society for the Abolition of Slavery purchased land from the Temne people. Slaves who were freed or who had escaped from the United States or the West Indies were welcomed to this land. Thousands of slaves who had been freed from slave ships by the British navy were also settled there. The region would become known as Sierra Leone.

In the 1800s Sierra Leone became a British crown *colony*. In 1961 it gained its independence.

R E V I E W

Directions:
Name the ethnic group or nation described by each statement.
1. This group lives in the southern part of Sierra Leone.
2. These descendants of freed slaves share Sierra Leone with the Mende and Temne ethnic groups.
3. This nation was founded by slaves freed by the British.
4. This nation was founded by freed slaves from the United States.
5. Rubber exports once made up the most important part of this nation's economy.
6. Once a British colony, this nation became independent in 1961.

SPOTLIGHT
S T O R Y

Letters from Gbassie

March 15, 1990

Dear American Pen Pal,

Happy Joseph Jenkins Roberts' Birthday! That's right. In Liberia, today is a national holiday. Ah, today will be a day to celebrate. Schools will be closed, and there will be music and dancing in the center of the town. We are celebrating the birthday of our first African American governor, Joseph Roberts. It is much like your celebration of George Washington's birthday in the United States.

Roberts was first appointed Governor of Liberia 157 years ago. He took over the government from a man named Thomas Buchanan, a cousin of your president, James Buchanan. In fact, Liberia's colonial period is very closely tied to the history of the United States. Did you know that the first colonists in Liberia were freed slaves from America? The first freed slaves arrived here in 1821. And did you know, my American friend, that our capital city, Monrovia, is named for your president, James Monroe?

My favorite Liberian instruments are the balang, the konny, and the *marimba*. The balang is what you Americans would call a guitar except that it has twenty-one strings! The konny is like a harp, and the marimba is just like a xylophone.

Tonight Mother will cook a feast for our entire family. Our family isn't really like most American families. When a person in Liberia says the word "family," he means all of his aunts, uncles, grandparents, and cousins. More than fifty people will eat with us this evening. You should be glad that you will not be eating with us because Liberian food is HOT!

Mother will cook everything with a lot of hot peppers. Whew! Once we had a dinner guest who was born in America. She liked the menu. Mother made a meal of monkey meat (she sometimes uses chickens or goats), greens, and palm oil cooked over rice. Our guest thought it looked fine— but did she ever have a surprise! I think Americans are just not used to peppers.

After supper, our whole family will go together to see our national team play a soccer game. Here in Liberia we call it football, and it is our national sport. There is not a boy or a man in Liberia who does not play soccer.

I will write to you again shortly.

Your Liberian friend,

Gbassie

July 26, 1990

Dear American Pen Pal,

Once again I write to you on a holiday. July 26th is our Independence Day. On this date in 1847, Joseph Jenkins Roberts became the first President of the first black republic in Africa.

And on this day one year ago, my older brother John returned from "Bush School." What is Bush School, you ask? Well, Bush School is a custom of the Poro people and of the Sande people. Both are religious societies. The Poro are men, and the Sande are women. The Bush Schools teach the children the customs and traditions of the different ethnic groups.

Young men spend four years away from home, and young women spend three. It is very rare to find a boy or a girl between the ages of twelve and fifteen in a village. They are away at Bush School to be taught by the *Zo*, who is the head teacher, and his helpers. At the end of Bush School, a boy or a girl is then a member of the Poro or of the Sande. He or she is then considered an adult. Some ethnic groups which are united by Poro and Sande societies are the Kepelle, the Loma, the Gola, and the Bandi.

Children from those ethnic groups go to regular school, too. However, when they get to be about twelve or so, they are taken into the great forests at night to be taught the ways of their people.

One ethnic group that is not a part of the Poro is the Mandingo. Perhaps you have read about the Mandingo? They are Muslims, and they do not like to mix with people from other ethnic groups. Mandingos are very tall, and you can tell them because of the long flowing robes that they wear. I don't wear a robe. Most days I just wear a pair of shorts and maybe a tee shirt. Shoes? Sometimes.

It is very hot in Liberia. The average temperature is almost eighty degrees. And, boy, does it rain a lot. Some parts of this country get 200 inches of rain a year! With all that rain, you can imagine that there are many farmers in my country. In fact, 90 percent of all the people here are farmers. They raise rice, palm trees, grapefruit, and butter pears. In your country you call "butter pears" avocados.

The farmers here also export coffee and bananas. But the chief crop here is rubber.

The Firestone Plantations Company, an American-owned firm, operates the largest rubber plantation in Liberia. Rubber trees are fascinating. They look like regular trees. But when a "tapper" cuts into the tree, the sap runs out. This sap is collected and made into rubber.

We also have beautiful woods in Liberia. *Mahogany*, red oak, and a tree called wismore grow in many of the forests. If you aren't a farmer in Liberia, you are probably a miner. There is much iron to be mined here and even some gold, diamonds, platinum, and lead.

I will write to you again soon.

Your friend,

Gbassie

Stop and Review
Read the two letters from Gbassie to his pen pal. Then, answer the following questions.
1. Tell three things that you might find in Liberia that would not find in your city.
2. Explain why you think Bush School is a good thing or a bad thing.
3. Find five things that are grown in Liberia.
4. List four things in Liberia that would not be new to you.
5. What is the name of the capital city of Liberia? Whom is it named after?
6. Describe two more ways in which Liberians and Americans share a common history.
7. Tell two things about Liberia's climate.
8. Name five foods eaten in Liberia. Be sure to include a meat selection that you find unusual.
9. What is the main cash crop of Liberia?

PART 4:
Guinea Coast Countries—
Ivory Coast, Ghana, Togo,
and Benin

Once the country called the Ivory Coast was a place where many, many elephants could be found. The tusks of elephants are made of ivory, a product greatly treasured in Europe and the United States. Now, most of the elephants are gone. During the colonial era, they were killed by the thousands for their tusks—some of which weighed up to 200 pounds each. However, the people of the Ivory Coast, called Ivorians, have many other resources to rely upon. Rich fertile soil and plenty of water make the Ivory Coast one of the most productive nations of the world. In fact, it has one of the most developed *economies* in Africa.

The Ivory Coast is located on the Gulf of Guinea. This country is bounded by Liberia, Guinea, Mali, Burkina Faso, and Ghana. The coastline extends for 315 miles, and neither *bay* nor cape breaks its regular shape. The coastal plain extends inland for about 40 miles. Beyond the coastal plain the land rises to a *plateau* with an elevation of more than 1,000 feet.

The climate near the coast is always warm and wet. The two rainy seasons are separated by less humid periods. In these coastal areas, the heat and rainfall create a tropical rain forest. On the plateaus, temperatures are lower due to the higher altitude, and there is a dry season. In the plateau region there is a low grass savanna.

The Ivory Coast chose to concentrate first on developing the agricultural segment before encouraging industry. This country is developing a strong market for its tropical agriculture products. It has made great efforts to increase such crops as pineapples, bananas, and sugar. Coffee and cacao production has been expanded. The Ivory Coast leads the world in the production of cacao and is third in coffee production.

Of course, the Ivorians still grow other typical African crops like millet, rice, groundnuts, and cassava. Another major crop in the Ivory Coast is timber. That's right! The Ivorian government treats timber as a crop. They plant and harvest trees just as many responsible tree-growers in America do: to protect the forest's future. The Ivory Coast leads Africa in the production of tropical *hardwoods*.

Oil—A New Industry

The Ivory Coast receives large amounts of money from foreign investors. As a result of this outside financing, the Ivory Coast has begun to produce oil. Enough oil comes from its off-shore wells to supply most of the country's needs.

Manufacturing strengthens the Ivory Coast's already strong economy. Goods manufactured include chemicals, aluminum, and automobiles.

The capital city of the Ivory Coast is Abidjan (ab i JAHN), This modern capital is a major port and also the location of many industries. Two other important cities are Bouake and Man. Most of the 7.5 million people in the Ivory Coast either live in small villages or in the country. French is the official language because the Ivory Coast was once a French colony. However, over 60 different languages are spoken.

Religions and Traditional Practices

Many ethnic groups live in this country. The largest is the Baule. Also living here are the Agni, the Dioula, the Ebrie, and a dozen other ethnic groups. About 60 percent of the people practice ethnic religions; about 25 percent are Muslims, and about 15 percent are Christian.

Ethnic religions are based on *animism*, the belief that spirits occupy all objects, both living and non-living. Some of these spirits are helpful while others are harmful. In traditional society, a priest or chief keeps his people in harmony with a combination of law, ritual, and magic.

Rush hour traffic in the city of Abidjan crosses over the Houphouet-Boigny Bridge, which was named for the Ivory Coast's progressive President.

A Strong and Stable Government

The president of the Ivory Coast since 1944 has been a man named Felix Houphouet-Boigny. He is responsible for the nation's political stability and for its economic development. He has been the only president the Ivory Coast has ever had.

The southern part of the Ivory Coast provides the best health conditions and services. Educational and job opportunities are also very good here. Many subsistence farmers are leaving the dry north to seek jobs in the cities and towns of the south.

Ghana's Past Glory

Possibly the earliest kingdom in sub-Sahara was the Empire of Ghana. This empire was at its greatest height from the 4th to the 11th centuries. It spread from the Atlantic Ocean to the Niger River and from the Sahara Desert south to below the Niger River. The capital city of Koumbi was described by an 11th century Arab historian El Bakri. Koumbi had as many as 30,000 people living within its walls. Archaeologists have uncovered evidence of a great civilization. The windows of the king's home were made of glass, a product that had not yet come into Europe at that time.

The Ghanians boasted, with good reason, that their university at Timbuktu was the oldest center of advanced learning in the world. Scholars from all parts of the known world came there to study.

Although most of the people of the Empire of Ghana were farmers, the power and wealth of Ghana depended on three resources—gold, salt, and iron. The Ghana, or ruler (the name "Ghana" comes from the ruler's title), controlled all the gold in the empire. Gold was so important that the word "ghana" itself came to mean gold. Salt was also vital to all the peoples and nations of the area. Iron was the vital metal used to produce weapons—spears, javelins, and swords. Ghana depended on the trans-Sahara trade in gold, salt, and iron for its very existence.

Modern Ghana

Ghana (GAHN uh) became an independent nation in 1957. This area was the first British colony in sub-Saharan Africa to gain independence.

The first elected leader to be head of the Ghana government was Kwame Nkrumah (KWAHM ee en KROO muh). He was a school teacher who had been educated in the United States. Upon his return to Ghana after his studies, he established a political party called the Convention People's Party.

Nkrumah proved to be a strong leader. He was an excellent politician and public speaker and gained the respect of all the peoples of his country. As a result of his enthusiasm, the people were willing to work very hard to achieve independence.

However, things quickly changed once Nkrumah became president. He made many policy changes. He increased his personal power and imprisoned some people who criticized the government. People began to fear the government. Many people felt that unwise decisions had damaged the economy and left the country with many large debts.

This government was overthrown in 1966 while Nkrumah was in China. A new National Liberation Council, headed by General Joseph Ankrah, ruled the country. Under this leadership, the country was returned to civilian rule.

Since that time, Ghana's political system has been unstable. The country has experienced *coups d'état* and has switched back and forth several times between civilian and military rule.

Modern Ghana's Economy

Cacao, which is used in making chocolate, continues to be an important cash-export crop for Ghana. However, due to the fall in world prices and to a government policy which neglected replanting, many farmers lost money and became discouraged.

Ghanians are famous for their wood carvings. Woodworkers are considered to be artists of the highest quality.

As a result, many Africans who had worked on the cacao plantations returned to their homes and traditional ways. Subsistence farming has increased greatly over the past 30 years. Ghana's farmers raise cassava, maize, millet, sorghum, and *yams.*

Dependence on one crop—cacao—has presented great problems. Attempts to diversify by setting up other industries have been partly successful. A great hydroelectric plant on the Volta River produces great amounts of electric power. A large aluminum plant, a steel mill, and an oil refinery have been built. Minerals such as bauxite for aluminum and manganese for steel, as well as gold and diamonds, are being mined.

Approximately 30 percent of Ghana's population live in cities. The

The Drums in Ghana

The oldest and best known object in the traditions of Ghana is the drum. It is used on social, military, and political occasions for talking, dancing, and singing. Drums are carved from the *kyendur* tree. Most are covered with the skin of a black antelope. The *atumpan* is a special ceremonial drum covered with elephant skin. They are large and "speak" great distances. To be skilled with the atumpan is a great honor for a Ghanaian.

capital city of Ghana is Accra (uh KRAH). This large, modern city has many shops, office buildings, restaurants, and banks. Most people get around Accra by walking or taking buses and taxis. Only a small percentage of the people own cars.

Although there are dozens of different ethnic groups in Ghana, most of the people are from a large group called the Akan. In Ghana, the Akan are split among two large groups, the Ashanti and the Fanti.

Togo and Benin

Togo (TOH goh) and Benin (buh NEEN) are small, hot, humid countries located on the Gulf of Guinea. Both countries are 90 percent agricultural. Almost all of the people of Togo and Benin live in villages or in the country. The crops grown there include cassava, millet, groundnuts, and palm oil. As in other countries along the Guinea Coast, coffee, cacao, and palm oil are important products.

The major ethnic groups in Togo are the Ewe and Cabrai. In Benin, the major groups include the Dahomeans, the Adja, and the Fulani.

Togo was a German colony before World War I (1914-1918). After the war, Britain ruled the western half of

Togo while France ruled the eastern half. In 1957 the people of the British Togo voted to become part of Ghana. French Togo became independent in 1960. Today, Togo has large phosphate reserves. That material, used to make fertilizers, has become the nation's largest export.

Benin was once a French protectorate called Dahomey. The French built a large school system but developed little of the country beyond its coast. The people of Benin rely on palm oil, peanuts, and cotton for income. At present there are not enough jobs for the people and many have left. The current name of the country comes from the Benin Kingdom that existed in West Africa during the 16th century.

Wildlife Preserves

Benin is also noted for a large wildlife *reserve*. The "W" National Park is a protected home for many animals native to Africa. You might see roans, hartebeests, gazelles, elephants, and hippopotamuses roaming free. The entire area of the "W" National Park covers almost 3 million acres of land, about half of which is located in Benin.

REVIEW

Directions:
Use complete sentences to answer the following questions.
1. What differences exist between developments in Ghana and the Ivory Coast since these countries gained independence?
2. How have the people of Ivory Coast attempted to improve their lives?
3. Why is the name "Ghana" important historically?
4. How have the colonial nations of Britain and France influenced the peoples of the Guinea Coast?
5. Why do you think the wildlife reserves are necessary in countries such as Benin?

MAP SKILLS

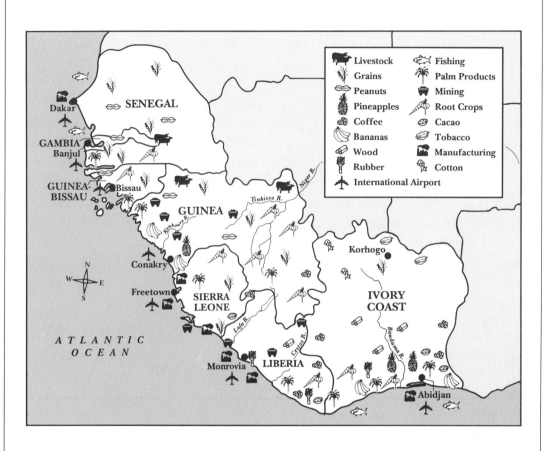

PRODUCTS OF COASTAL WEST AFRICA

1. What types of trees are grown near the mouth of the Cestos River in Liberia?
2. What two crops are grown near Korhogo in the Ivory Coast?
3. Name three cities in which one might find an international airport.
4. Which product is not to be found near Freetown in Sierra Leone: palm products, mining, fishing, or manufacturing?
5. Name three products found near the Tinkisso River in Guinea.
6. Name two countries in which peanuts can be found.

CHAPTER 1 REVIEW

Summary of Coastal West Africa

Coastal West Africa is a land of many different people. Hundreds of ethnic groups, languages, and customs exist. Yet the people of Coastal West Africa have much in common. All 11 countries in this region share the same type of agriculture, history, and traditions. All are still considered to be developing countries.

Much history has happened in this area of the world. Great empires like the Ghana and Ashanti have flourished. The trading of slaves was also a part of the history of West Africa.

Critical Thinking Skills

Directions: Give some serious thought to the questions below. Be sure to answer in complete sentences.

1. How do you think that the official language of Guinea came to be French?
2. Why is it important for a young man in Liberia to attend Bush School?
3. Why do countries like Togo and Benin rely so heavily on farming?
4. In his letters to an American pen pal, why is Gbassie so proud of Joseph Jenkins Roberts?
5. How do you think the farmers of Coastal West Africa are different from American farmers?

Write It!

Directions: Read the selection below. In a short paragraph, explain what the words of Nkrumah mean to you.

Ghana was the first colonial nation in Africa to win its independence. The area became a colony of Great Britain in 1874 and was given the name "Gold Coast." On March 6, 1957, under the leadership of Kwame Nkrumah, the Gold Coast became independent and took the name of the ancient kingdom described earlier in this chapter. On that day Nkrumah offered the following prophetic words.

"There is a new African in the world, and that new African is ready to fight his own battles....It is the only way in which we can show the world we are the masters of our own destiny."

For Discussion

Directions: Discuss these questions with your class. Appoint one class member to write the ideas you discover on the board.

1. If a farmer from Ghana came to this country, what things would he want to take home with him?
2. Most of the countries in Coastal West Africa were once colonies of a European nation. How does this affect the way in which they presently live?
3. Water is an especially important commodity in Africa. Think of ways in which a farmers's life is different in times of drought.
4. What difficulties might a tourist have in traveling through the areas of Coastal West Africa?
5. What popular American foods are probably not eaten in Coastal West Africa and why? Hint: Hot dogs are not eaten because they are pork, and pigs are not raised in this area of the world. Eating pork is also forbidden by the Muslim religion.

For You To Do

Directions: Make a chart of the countries of Coastal West Africa. Be sure to include population and types of government on your chart. Use colors to depict the flags of each country. You can find this information in an encyclopedia.

CENTRAL WEST AFRICA

F A C T S

- Equatorial Guinea consists of land on the mainland plus five *islands*.
- Cameroon has over 250 miles (400 kilometers) of coastline.
- About 11 million people live in Cameroon; 110 million live in Nigeria.
- Nigeria became an independent nation in 1960.
- Nigeria produces large amounts of cacao, peanuts, rubber, and oil.

PART 1:
Nigeria—A Proud History

Compared to the other nations of West Africa, Nigeria (ny JIR ee uh) is enormous. With more than 110 million people, it is the most populated country in all of Africa. One out of every five Africans lives in Nigeria. Population experts predict that by the year 2100, Nigeria will have the world's third largest population—500 million people.

Nigeria extends from the wet, hot climate of the coast on the Gulf of Guinea to the dry *savannas* along Lake Chad. In the tropical south, palm products, *cacao,* and rubber are grown. In the drier savannas of the north, peanuts, cotton, soybeans, and cattle are raised. However, in the central region, the *tsetse* fly and the resulting sleeping sickness prevent the development of *agriculture* and the raising of cattle.

Nigeria is the home of the mighty Niger (Ny jur) River. The Niger, which has its *source* in the highlands of Guinea, flows for 2,600 miles. Two

CENTRAL WEST AFRICA

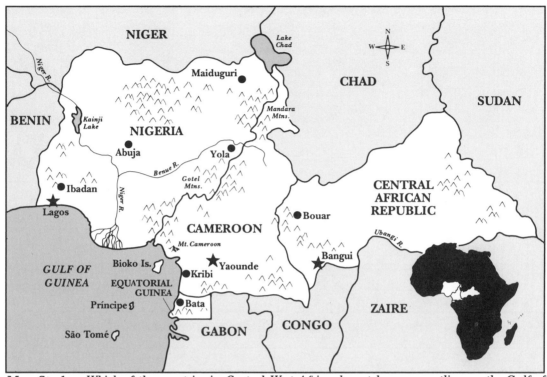

Map Study: *Which of the countries in Central West Africa do not have a coastline on the Gulf of Guinea? Which two countries share a border with Chad? In which country can you find Kainji Lake? Near which body of water is Mt. Cameroon? Which country in Central West Africa is closest to the islands of Príncipe and São Tomé?*

other major rivers—the Benue, which is a *tributary* or branch of the Niger River, and the Komodugu-Yobe in the north—are also found in Nigeria.

Nigeria is one of the richest countries in Africa. Its greatest mineral resources are the large oil deposits of the Niger River *delta* region. This oil brings a new wealth to some Nigerians who work in the petroleum industry. Unfortunately, only a small portion of the people share in the wealth that oil brings. The majority of Nigerians live in villages. In fact, 75 percent of the people of Nigeria still cannot read or write.

Coal deposits are also found in this delta area. Located inland are large iron ore and manganese mines. Nigeria has about half of the world's supply of *columbite*, a metal used in hardening steel. On the Niger River, a large hydroelectric plant has been built that will supply electric power for homes and industry.

More than two-thirds of the people are farmers. They grow *yams, cassava, millet,* corn, and rice as food crops. Their *export* crops include cacao, rubber, and palm products. Unfortunately, *drought* has been a serious problem for Nigeria's farmers.

Lagos (LAY gohs), the capital of Nigeria, is one of the largest cities. However, Lagos is overcrowded, and many of its people cannot find work. Lagos is really two cities in one. The "old" city suffers from poor sanitary conditions and polluted water. The "new" Lagos is a well-planned, modern city with office buildings, luxury hotels, restaurants, and universities.

To reduce the dominance of Lagos and to relieve its problems, a new capital is being set up in the modern city of Abuja in the center of Nigeria. In the north, walled cities such as Kano have been religious and trading centers for prosperous Muslim kingdoms of the past. Today, Kano is still an important cultural, religious, and trade center as well as the largest city of the north. Ibadan (i BAHD un) is another important city of southeastern Nigeria.

Nigerians Belong to Many Different Ethnic Groups

As in other African nations, the people of Nigeria belong to many *ethnic groups* that have developed cultural differences. Nigerians trace their ancestry to one of more than 250 language and ethnic groups. Four major groups include the Hausa, the Fulani, the Yoruba, and the Ibo.

The Hausa people of Nigeria grow large amounts of groundnuts. In the United States, groundnuts are called peanuts.

The Yoruba of the Lagos-Ibadan region and the Ibo of the lower Niger River region of the southeast have been most influenced by the English. Many of the southern Nigerians speak English, which is the official language of the government. Most of them practice Christianity.

The two large groups of the north include the Hausa, who make up one-fifth of the people of Nigeria, and the Fulani. These and most of the other people in the northern region are *Muslims* who have maintained traditional culture. In fact, 47 percent of the people of Nigeria are Muslims. Throughout the country, however, many Nigerians combine Muslim or Christian religious practices with traditional beliefs. Their beliefs are often based on the worship of many gods and spirits. (See Spotlight Story for this chapter).

Each of the four large ethnic groups in Nigeria is distrustful of the others. Each has its own customs, religion, and language. English is the national language because it is not the language of any single group. A *civil war* broke out in 1967 when the Ibo tried to set up an independent country, Biafra. The war ended in 1970 when the Biafrans were defeated.

This impressive ancient terra-cotta head was sculpted over 1800 years ago. The head is almost life-size.

Culture in Nigeria

Nigeria has a proud history. Advanced cultures appeared in what is present-day Nigeria between 900 B.C. and A.D. 200 At that time, the Nok *culture* flourished. Working with *terra-cotta* clay, Nok artists sculpted nearly life-sized human figures. About A.D. 1000, the Ife made magnificent glazed pottery figures. These people also produced *bronze* portraits that rank among the world's finest sculpture. During the 14th century, bronze workers in Benin (buh NEEN) developed the "lost wax process" to create spectacular bronze figures and plaques. This art of early Africa has influenced many European and African artists of today.

Nigerians continue to enjoy worldwide fame as skilled artists. Yoruba and Ibo artists have contributed beautiful sculpture and very high quality modern artwork to museums throughout the world.

The African "talking drum," which is found in Western Nigeria, has an hourglass shape and is covered on the top and bottom by animal skins held together with leather bands. The drummer holds the drum under his left arm and hits the top of it with a stick held in his right hand. The sounds of the drum are like the tones of speech that people use. The Ibo, the Fulani, and the Hausa are known for their music, instruments, and dances.

Let's Play!

The people in Nigeria are just like anyone else in Africa and in the rest of the world—they like to have fun.

Nigerians enjoy many sports both as spectators and participants. Wrestling, soccer, polo, football (American-style), cricket, and swimming are all very popular.

Nigerians also have a love for the movies. Because most Nigerians speak English, most movies are in that language. Nigerians know all about Eddie Murphy, Roger Rabbit, and Rocky. In addition to the movies, live theater and art exhibits are well attended in Nigeria. Don't forget TV. Several television stations currently broadcast in Nigeria.

R E V I E W

Directions:
Choose the correct word or words from the chapter to match each definition.
1. A branch of a major river
2. A metal used to make steel harder
3. An industry built near water to supply electric power
4. A group that makes up one-fifth of the people of Nigeria
5. A method of creating bronze figures

PART 2:
Cameroon—
Lowlands, Marshes, and Plains

Cameroon (kam uh ROON) is a triangle-shaped country that is located near the bend in West Africa. It has approximatelyt 250 miles of coastline on the Gulf of Guinea. Cameroon's capital city is Yaounde (yauun DAY). It has two official languages—English and French.

Many different types of land are located in Cameroon. You can find *tropical* lowlands; flooded *marshes*; forested mountain ranges; and broad, flat *grasslands*. A large amount of *rain forests* also exist in Cameroon. These tropical forests are very humid (hot and wet). They are also very dense. Within the forests, you will find plants and vines growing very close to each other. The rain forests are so dense that light can barely pass through them, and they are dark most of the time. In these vast forests grow magnificent *hardwood* trees like *mahogany* and *ebony*. Many different types of beautiful and *exotic* flowers also grow in Cameroon.

Wildlife Is Plentiful

This country also supports many different types of wildlife. Although hunters have made their numbers smaller, a wide variety of African animals call Cameroon their home. Some animals living in this country are rhinoceroses, monkeys of all kinds, large pythons, elephants, flying mice, and even lions. There are also crocodiles, gorillas, cheetahs, leopards, giraffes, hippopotamuses, buffaloes, and antelopes. Many of these animals now live on protected wildlife *preserves*. Cameroon has six of these preserves.

Peoples of Cameroon

Today, about 11 million people live in Cameroon. The largest ethnic group is the Fulani. These people are Muslims who have fought religious wars against members of other groups who follow traditional African religions. Other people that live in Cameroon include the Bantu, the Bamileke, and the southern groups such as the Ibo, the Ibidio, and the Edo.

One group of people who are smaller than average also live in Cameroon. They are commonly known as pygmies, even though the term is incorrect. Several groups of these unique people share similar physical characteristics. The three largest groups are the Mbuti, the Aka, and the Efe. These people live in the forest and are primarily hunters.

Most people in this area make their living as farmers. Cameroon exports coffee, cacao, bananas, wood, cotton, tea, and rubber. Other crops include cassava, corn, yams, rice, and sweet potatoes. Cattle are raised in the highland regions away from the coast.

Industries include *bauxite,* iron ore, and food processing as well as light manufacturing, lumbering, and production of crude oil.

Further development of commercial farming and mineral resources promises continued economic growth for Cameroon.

R E V I E W

Directions:
Write *True* or *False* for each statement.
1. Most of Cameroon's coastline borders the Atlantic Ocean.
2. Two valuable hardwoods found in the forests of Cameroon include mahogany and ebony.
3. The official language of Cameroon is Portuguese.
4. Coffee and cacao are two important export products for Cameroon.
5. Many wild animals of Cameroon are protected on preserves.

SPOTLIGHT
S T O R Y

Religion in Africa

Although many Africans are Muslims or Christians, the majority of ethnic peoples still follow traditional religions. Most traditional religions profess a belief in one supreme God. However, this God in most cases can be reached only through ancestors or spirits. Many Africans believe that everything has a spirit—the trees in the forest, stones, animals, and rivers. These powerful spirits can influence people's lives. If a spirit is angry, it can take revenge. Therefore, if a person moves a stone, he or she must be careful to do something to keep the spirit of the stone from becoming angry. Such beliefs are known as *animism.*

Spirits and ancestors can influence people's lives. Usually an ethnic group has one spirit that is of greatest importance to it. This spirit serves as the go-between among group members and the supreme God. The group usually makes special offerings or sacrifices to the spirit to keep its favor. There are also taboos, or things that should not be done for fear of angering the spirits. If the group should lose the spirit's favor, catastrophic events could occur. Spirits might differ in name or importance from group to group or village to village, but they are thought to be all-powerful throughout most of sub-Sahara Africa.

Magic is basically the idea that supernatural forces can be controlled and used by human beings. This belief is widely held throughout Africa. The force of magic can be used for good or evil. In Africa most magic is used with good intent. It is used to protect persons against illness and misfortune. It is used to guarantee success in farming, fishing, hunting, or even love. In fact, one of the most important functions of magic is to give people extra confidence in difficult situations that they cannot entirely control.

An individual who can control this magic is of great importance and holds great power within the group. Someone who has displeased a spirit must go to a *shaman* (SHAY mun *or* SHAH mun). This person is one who is able to overpower negative or harmful forces. Traditional African belief sees a close connection between the spirit world and the diseases that affect people. The shaman bridges that connection. He renames the spirit, and the person is well again. The shaman's cures, portents (views of the future), and advice are protective devices.

Traditional ethnic religions are gradually giving way to Christianity and Islam—though probably not more than 40 percent of sub-Saharan Africans would regard themselves as either Christians or Muslims. Furthermore, some converts to these religions also cling in private to traditional beliefs and rituals. Many Africans see no conflict in holding their new beliefs and their traditional beliefs at the same time.

Stop and Review

Answer the following questions in complete sentences.

1. What is animism?
2. What is a taboo?
3. Describe two ways in which magic is used with good intent.
4. Who is a shaman? How does the shaman help the people?
5. What is happening to traditional ethnic beliefs in Africa today? Explain your answer.

PART 3:
The Central African Republic and Equatorial Guinea

The Central African *Republic* is a poor country, even less developed than many of its neighbors. Its people suffer from many problems. Many of the citizens of the Central African Republic do not live to be 50 years old. One cause of disease and death is an insect. The tsetse fly spreads sleeping sickness, a disease that takes the lives of many of the people in this area.

Much of the Central African Republic is inhabited by wildlife. Seven wildlife preserves are in this country. The land supports great herds of antelopes, buffaloes, lions, rhinoceroses, gorillas, and elephants. Perhaps the largest remaining elephant herds in the world today can be found in the Central African Republic.

Peoples of Central African Republic

People in the Central African Republic belong to many different ethnic groups. Among them are the Banda, the Baya, the Ubangi, the Sara, and the Mandjia. The Ubangi live along the Ubangi River, which is a chief waterway in the Central African Republic.

About 80 ethnic and language groups—most of them Bantu-speakers—make up the population of the Central African Republic. About one-fourth of the people are Roman Catholics, one-fourth are Protestant, and one-tenth are Muslim. The rest of the people practice their own traditional African religions.

Art and Literature in the Central African Republic

Many Central African artists work in watercolors and in oils. In the large villages and cities of this country, it is customary to see many paintings and murals done by local artists. These art works can usually be seen in restaurants, bars, and other gathering places.

Jerome Ramedane is the most famous artist from this region. Ramedane's murals and canvasses often show African animal life, daily village life, and hunting parties.

Literature in Central Africa is starting to become more popular. Collectors are beginning to gather and record the region's traditional oral legends and folk tales. Pierre Makombo Bambote is the most renowned writer in the Central African Republic. His work is a source of great pride to the people of his country.

Mining is the only major industry in Central Africa that is not farm-related. This area of Africa is a major source of industrial diamonds. They are found in rock formations deep in the earth. The rock where diamonds are found is called blue ground. Many tons of blue ground must be carefully sorted through to find one diamond. Miners use special equipment when searching for diamonds.

Many Natural Resources

The Central African Republic is trying to build up its *economy*. It has many natural resources, including diamonds, that have become major non-farming industries. The country also supplies most of its own food.

Crops include cassavas, potatoes, rice, *sorghum*, peanuts, and bananas—all of which are traded at local markets. Cotton, coffee, and sesame are cash-export crops. In addition, diamonds and timber are important export products.

Almost all of the farming in this country is done by women. The men do the hunting and fishing. In Central Africa, it is not considered honorable for a grown man to work in the fields.

Akwadu
(Banana-Coconut Bake)

Akwadu is a typical West African dessert. Its basic ingredients, bananas and coconuts, are both grown in the area. Just as baseball is "as American as apple pie," soccer is "as African as akwadu."

5 medium bananas
1 tablespoon butter
1/3 cup orange juice
1 tablespoon lemon juice

3 tablespoons packed brown sugar
2/3 cup shredded coconut

Cut bananas crosswise into halves; cut each piece in half. Arrange bananas in an ungreased 9-inch pie pan. Dot with butter. Drizzle with orange and lemon juice. Sprinkle with brown sugar and coconut. Heat oven to 375 degrees and bake 8 to 10 minutes or until coconut is golden brown.

Equatorial Guinea

Equatorial Guinea (ee kwuh TOHR ee ul GIN ee) is a very small country whose population is under a half million. Most of the people of Equatorial Guinea belong to an ethnic group known as the Foulah.

Most of the land in Equatorial Guinea contains dense rain forests. The hardwood grown there is a major product that is exported to other countries. Along the shoreline lies flat land where the people of Equatorial Guinea grow cacao, coffee, and bananas. These products are also exported.

Equatorial Guinea promotes African culture through lectures and exhibits. In the city of Bata is a museum of art that has the works of Guinea's internationally known sculptor, Leandro Mbomio.

R E V I E W

Directions:
Use information from the text to help you complete the following sentences.
1. The _____ is an insect which spreads African sleeping sickness.
2. The important _____ River flows through the Central African Republic.
3. _____ may be the home of the largest herd of elephants in the world today.
4. Jerome Ramedane is a famous _____ from the Central African Republic.
5. A museum of art located in _____ displays some of the works of sculptor Leandro Mbomio.

MAP SKILLS

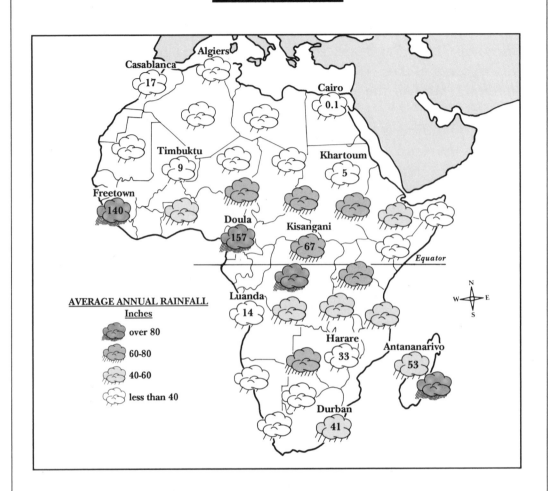

AVERAGE ANNUAL RAINFALL IN AFRICA

1. What is the average amount of annual rainfall in Luanda?

2. What southern African city receives 41 inches of rainfall per year?

3. What is the average annual rainfall in Doula?

4. Which part of Africa receives the greatest amount of annual rainfall?

5. What city near the equator receives 67 inches of rain per year?

6. Which part of Africa receives the least amount of annual rainfall?

CHAPTER 2 REVIEW

Summary of Central West Africa

Central West Africa includes one of the largest and one of the smallest countries in all of Africa. It is also home to the smallest people in the world. Animals actually outnumber the people in this area. Thousands upon thousands of animals roam its broad, flat grasslands. If you traveled in this part of the world, you would see great herds of antelopes, elephants, buffaloes, and giraffes. Also living here are lions, leopards, hippos, rhinos, and monkeys of all kinds.

Critical Thinking Skills

Directions: Give some serious thought to the questions below. Be sure to answer in complete sentences.

1. Explain why the culture of groups such as the Mbuti have remained unchanged for hundreds of years.
2. Why do you think so many animals live in the grasslands of Central West Africa?
3. Why do you think so many of the people in this area live along the banks of the Ubangi River?
4. Why are the numbers of so many wild animals getting smaller and smaller?
5. Look at the map of Central West Africa in this chapter. Why do you think Nigeria is not home to many herds of wild animals?

Write It!

Directions: Many Westerners take photo safaris to this part of the world to "shoot" the animals. Describe the animals, plants, and other natural features that a photographer might look for on the grasslands of Cameroon.

For Discussion

Directions: Discuss these questions with your class. Appoint one class member to write the ideas you discover on the board.

1. How do the people near the coastline live differently from their inland countrymen?
2. What are some of the reasons that many things grow so large and so fast in the rain forests?
3. List at least three reasons why people tend to live near a source of water.
4. Indicate some similarities and some differences between the Mbuti of Central West Africa and the 19th century American Indians of the United States.
5. In what ways is Nigeria different from its neighboring countries?

For You To Do

Directions: Go to the library to find books of recipes. Use the table of contents and the index to find traditional African recipes like Akwadu. Copy these recipes. Then, tell which ingredients are easy to get and which are difficult to find in America. Perhaps it would be interesting if someone at home helped you prepare a recipe in traditional African style.

EQUATORIAL WEST AFRICA

F	• Equatorial West Africa is extremely rich in natural resources.
A	• The Congo River is the fifth longest river in the world.
C	• Rainfall in Gabon may reach 100 inches in a nine-month period.
T	• Wearing Western-styled clothing is discouraged in Zaire.
S	• Margherita Peak in Zaire towers 16,762 feet high.

PART 1:
Land of Many Contrasts

E quatorial West Africa is an area of many contrasts. The countries in this area include some of the smallest and some of the largest in Africa. The people, too, are among the smallest and the largest in the world. In Equatorial West Africa are dense *tropical rain forests* and breathtaking coastlines. The countries are a mixture of poverty and of wealth.

Only a few cities can be found in Equatorial Africa. Most of the people live in small villages scattered about the countryside. The people in these villages are usually farmers. The houses are made from *adobe* bricks or dried mud and sticks. Many have thatched roofs—that is, roofs made of dried bundles of grass. Wealthier families might have a house made with a tin roof.

Gabon

Gabon (ga BOHN) is a coastal country that lies almost directly on the *equator*. Between June and

EQUATORIAL WEST AFRICA

Map Study: *Which countries in this region do not border on the coast of the Atlantic Ocean? In which country do you find lakes named Mweru, Tanganyika, and Mobutu Sese Seko? Which country shares a border with Namibia and Zambia? Which two countries have their capital cities located on the Congo River? Which two countries are separated by the Ubangi River?*

rain forests are a haven to many species of wild animals. Gorillas, monkeys, leopards, and tropical birds of all kinds thrive within the rain forests of Gabon.

The rain forests also play a major part in the *economy* of the area. Rich *hardwoods* are harvested from the rain forests. These beautiful hardwoods, such as *ebony* and *mahogany,* are the chief *exports* of this relatively rich nation. Two other exports include *cacao* and coffee beans.

Additionally, the Gabonese export valuable iron, *uranium,* oil, gold, and manganese. As a result, this nation has a trade surplus. The country has been able to use the money to improve education and health facilities. The government of Gabon is also developing a new railway and new roads leading to the mines and farms in the interior.

September, it rarely rains in this country. However, during the other nine months, rainfall may reach 100 inches. Much of Gabon contains thick tropical rain forest with little light; thick vines limit ground travel. As *inhospitable* as this may seem, these

Gabon's capital city is called Libreville (LEE bruh vil). Approximately 115,000 people live there. Although this is a small city by American standards, it is not considered a small city by African standards. Many of the people of Gabon live in cities. This kind of population distribution is unusual for a country in Africa.

The Volcanic Islands of São Tomé and Príncipe

São Tomé (sauut uh MAY) and Príncipe (PRIN suh pay) are two small islands just off the coast of Gabon. Both are *volcanic islands*. They are actually large volcanoes rising out of the sea. They are about 80 miles apart. The capital city of this unique two-island nation is the city of São Tomé.

The temperature of the two islands ranges from 66 degrees F. to 89 degrees F. This range of temperatures is perfect for growing sugarcane and coffee. São Tomé and Príncipe grow a lot of cacao. Palm oil and bananas are exported to other countries.

The islands were first inhabited by the Portuguese in the fifteenth century. For many years the islands were used as stopping-off points for the shipment of slaves to Western

countries. Later on, the population grew substantially with a new wave of Portuguese convicts and Jewish *refugees*.

The Republic of the Congo and the Congo River

The *Republic* of the Congo (KAHN goh) is a land dominated by the Congo River. Much of the transportation, energy, and economy of this area depend on this river.

The Congo River is the largest river in Africa. However, it is not the longest river. The longest river in Africa is the Nile River. More water flows through the Congo than through the Nile. In all the world, only the Amazon River in South America carries more water. The waters of the Congo River are a rusty color. This coloring is caused by the tremendous amounts of *silt* carried by its waters.

The capital city of the Congo is Brazzaville (BRAZ uh vil). French was adopted as the official language in order not to favor one people's speech. However, most of the Congolese speak a *Bantu* language. Among these languages are Swahili, Lingula, and Mono Kutuba.

The *ethnic groups* of the Congo are almost all of Bantu origin. They include the Bakongo, the Brazzaville, the Songha, and the Teke. Hutus live in the rain forests of the Congo.

The Republic of the Congo is a hot, humid place. Being so near the equator means that the temperature year round is near 90 degrees. The tropical rain forests of the Congo are rich. They are home to many types of monkeys, cobras, and pythons. Also found in the rain forests are *exotic* plants and valuable trees. The Congolese harvest and export oak, cedar, mahogany, and walnut trees.

Away from the rain forests, the land becomes a thick, grassy *plain.* This type of land, known as *savanna,* is home to lions, elephants, buffaloes, leopards, giraffes, and zebras.

Three out of every four people in the Congo make their living as farmers. They raise *sorghum,* sweet potatoes, and corn. Larger farms grow and export coffee, rubber, cotton, sugarcane, bananas, cacao, and palm oil.

Mining for copper is a mainstay of the economy of this region. Huge strip mines are dug to expose the copper that is hidden in the ground.

The Republic of the Congo is also rich in minerals. The Congolese mine copper, gold, and silver that are exported to other countries. The country also has oil, natural gas, and potash deposits. Projects supported by foreign aid have built hydroelectric stations and *textile* miles. A shipyard in the port city of Pointe-Noire has also been built.

R E V I E W

Directions:

Answer in complete sentences.

1. What materials are used to build houses in Equatorial West Africa? Why are houses made with these materials?
2. What are some natural resources found in Gabon?
3. About how many years ago did the Portuguese first inhabit the islands of Principé and São Tomé?
4. Why is the Congo region so hot and humid?
5. Why do you think most of the large cities of Congo and Gabon are located either on the coast or along a river?

PART 2:
Angola—Torn by War

Angola (an GOH luh) is one of the largest countries in Africa. However, it has one of the smallest populations with fewer than 10 million people living in Angola today. Many reasons contribute to this small population. For instance, in colonial times, millions of Africans were captured and sent to be traded as slaves. More recently, warfare among various political parties has kept the population of Angola small.

Of the 10 million people that do live in Angola, most live on farms or in the countryside. Farmers produce bananas, coffee, *cassava*, sugarcane, and *sisal*. Sisal is used to make ropes.

Angola has many natural resources. A large oil field is near Cabinda (kuh BIN duh) in the northeastern part of the nation. Angola also mines and exports diamonds, iron, and aluminum. Recently, gold was discovered in this country.

Angola is a land of many rivers. Some of the rivers flow north to the Congo River, and some flow west to the Atlantic Ocean. Two of the larger rivers in Angola are the Zambezi (zam BEE zee) and Cunene (koo NAY nuh) Rivers.

Angola Was Once the Jewel of Colonial Portugal

Hundreds of years ago Europeans made their first contacts with people from Africa. At first, the Europeans came across the Mediterranean Sea and into Egypt. These visitors traveled as far as the Sahara and could go no farther.

About 550 years ago, the Spanish and the Portuguese began to explore the west coast of Africa. There they discovered many riches. They found fruits, nuts, palm oil, ivory, spices, and gold. They also found a source of slave labor to send to the new world.

The Portuguese were particularly drawn to the area of what is now called Angola. They fought for centuries to make it a Portuguese *colony* (which it became in 1901). However, this domination of the people of western Africa did not last for long. The Angolans fought fiercely for their independence, and Angola became an independent nation in 1974.

Ethnic Differences and Civil War

Many different African ethnic groups make their homes in Angola. Unfortunately, relations among the larger groups have not always been good. *Civil war* has been a fact of life in Angola for many years.

Four major ethnic groups live in Angola today. They are the Ovimbundu, the Mbundu, the Bakongo, and the Lunda-Chokwe. Most of the members of the groups speak the Bantu language. However, Portuguese is the official language of Angola. It is spoken mainly by the remaining whites whose ancestors lived in Angola when it was a Portuguese colony.

Angola's civil war is based on ethnic differences. In the north people are closely related to groups in Zaire. In the south people are related to groups in Namibia. The southern people support a guerrilla group that is trying to overthrow the central government.

The government in the capital of Luanda (luu AN duh) enjoys support from the peoples living in the center of Angola. The Luanda government has adopted a socialist-communist economic and political policy. Troops from Cuba were used to help fight against the rebels. These Cuban troops left Angola early in 1989.

Until there is peace within the country and a stable government has been put in place, Angola cannot prosper.

R E V I E W

Directions:
Use the text to help you complete the following sentences.
1. Angola was at one time a colony of _____.
2. A plant product used to produce rope is _____.
3. Two important African rivers located in Angola are the _____ and _____.
4. Most of the people of Angola speak _____.
5. A war between groups of people within a single country is called a _____.

EQUATORIAL WEST AFRICA

PART 3:
Zaire—Rich in Resources

Zaire (ZEYE ur) is located directly on the equator. The ethnic groups of this country are almost all of Bantu origin. Although the official language is French, most people speak one of four regional languages.

Zaire is dependent on its largest river, the Congo River. The Zairians call it the Zaire River. The capital city, Kinshasa (kin SHAHS uh), is found along the banks of the Zaire River. This river provides transportation, energy, and water for crops.

Zaire is actually made up of three different regions in one country: the rain forest, the savannas, and the mountains.

Rain Forests

Most of Zaire is a tropical rain forest. It is much like the other rain forests that you have read about: thick, dark, and humid. Because this country is so close to the equator, its rain forest is particularly hot. The average daytime temperature in this region is 90 degrees.

The Zairian rain forest supports a tremendous variety of plant life. Beautiful hardwood trees grow there, as do palm trees and rubber trees.

Many different types of wild animals also live in the forests of Zaire. Pythons, chimpanzees, and crocodiles all live within the forest.

The Savannas and Highlands

Zaire is a place of vast savannas. These wide grassy lands are dotted with small groves of trees. The *grasslands* make a perfect home for many of the animals you might expect to see in Africa. Herds of antelopes, zebras, buffaloes, giraffes, rhinoceroses, hippopotamuses, and cats of every kind live in this area.

Large parts of Zaire have been set aside by the government to protect these wild animals. Hunters and a growing population are both threats to the wildlife of the area. Still, huge numbers of animals are found away from the places where people live.

Zaire has a mountainous highland where summits rise over 16,000 feet. Near the eastern border, at the top of Mount Zaire, is Margherita Peak. It is 16,762 feet high.

Crops and Natural Resources

Zaire is rich in natural resources. Much of the land is unused and has the largest hardwood reserves in Africa. This nation also has the ability and the resources to supply electrical power for the entire country as well as many of its neighbors.

Most of Zaire's economic development has been focused on the mining industry. In fact, mining has become the most important economic activity. Zaire is one of the world's largest producers of copper. Huge, open pit copper mines can be found in the southeastern regions. Deposits of *cobalt,* gold, and tin are also found nearby. Even oil has been found off Zaire's Atlantic coast.

Zaire needs money from outside sources to develop its economy. Consequently, much of the focus is on producing crops that can be exported. One exported product is palm oil, which is used as an ingredient in soap. Exported food crops include coffee and cocoa.

Education Is a Priority

Zaire's goal is to provide all of its citizens with a basic education. In 1980, over 80 percent of boys and 55 percent of girls were enrolled in school. Students not only learn to read, but they also study up-to-date science and technology. Providing an education for its people is challenging for the government because there is a shortage of secondary schools, especially in the rural areas. Youths are moving to the cities in hopes of getting a good education.

Art and Music

People from all over the world are familiar with Zaire's statues,

Education is a high priority in Zaire and other African states. The Lovnaium University at Kinshasa contributes to the higher education of Africans in Zaire as well as surrounding areas.

ivory carvings, masks, and jewelry. In fact, art from all parts of Zaire can be found in many major museums in the world. As an individual goal, Zaire has made an attempt to collect and preserve the art of the country's various peoples.

Music also plays an important role in a Zairian's life. The people sing songs in several languages, including French and the African languages of Kongo and Luba. The most widely used language is Lingala, which is not associated with any Zairian ethnic group. Lingala used to be the official language of the army, but now it is only associated with music.

Most Zairian songs are about the daily aspects of life: love, death, lack of money, as well as world problems. The most famous musician in Zaire is a man named Tabu Ley. He and his band, African International, have performed in the United States, Japan, and Europe.

Zaire's Recent History

Zaire was at one time called the Belgian Congo. In June of 1960, Zaire became independent. The idea of a united country was not widely supported. The peoples of Zaire often thought first of their own ethnic group, traditional *culture,* and welfare of their own area. After independence, political parties battled to control the government. A civil war broke out. After several changes of government, the commander of the army, a man named Mobutu Sese Seko, took total control. Mobutu has ruled the country since that time.

Despite the vast base of natural resources, the government of Zaire has not been able to meet all the needs and desires of the Zairian people. As a result, the country must *import* consumer goods, mining and transportation equipment, and fuels. To pay for these items, Zaire depends on foreign loans and aid.

R
E
V
I
E
W

Directions:
Write *True* or *False* for each statement.
1. The Congo River plays an important role in the life of the people of Zaire.
2. Zaire was once called the Portuguese Congo.
3. Areas located near the equator support little or no plant life.
4. Zaire has a rich tradition of art and music.
5. The country of Zaire was peaceful after gaining its independence.

SPOTLIGHT
S T O R Y

Family Life in Equatorial Africa

Africans are people who usually live as families. Some families are extended to include uncles, aunts, grandparents, and cousins. Some families even include more than one wife. The family forms the building blocks of society.

According to tradition, many girls in Africa are brought up differently from girls in America. African girls are brought up to be very dedicated to their husbands. They are also taught to have the highest respect for their fathers and uncles. Later they are trained to treat all men with great respect. Until recently, girls rarely went to school. Some Africans reasoned that girls were destined to work in the fields, serve their husbands, raise a family, and run a household. Today, however, many African girls learn to read and write.

Many girls from this region marry when they are twelve years old, and most marry before they are fifteen. Sixteen-year-old girls who are still unmarried are called "old maids." It is traditional for a bride's family to receive a *dowry* when she marries. Often a young girl marries a man who already has a wife. This practice, called *polygyny,* is common in Africa.

Boys are raised differently in this part of the world, too. Great importance is placed upon the traditions of the ethnic group. Boys are taught to hunt, trap, fish, and farm. They learn how to make weapons and tools, skin an animal, and find water. Storytelling is also the job of the male in African society. When they are teenagers, African boys undergo a "coming of age" ceremony. The boys are taken from their village and taught in a very intense manner about the customs and traditions of their tribe. At the end of the ceremony, each boy is then considered to be a man among his peers.

Stop and Review
Use complete sentences to answer the questions.
1. List four traditional duties that boys are expected to fulfill in Equatorial West Africa.
2. How are the lives of young girls in Equatorial West Africa different from lives of girls in your city?
3. How might you compare the lives of boys in Equatorial West Africa to the lives of boys in the United States?
4. Which relatives are considered part of the African family?
5. Until recently, why were African girls usually not educated in schools?

EQUATORIAL WEST AFRICA

MAP SKILLS

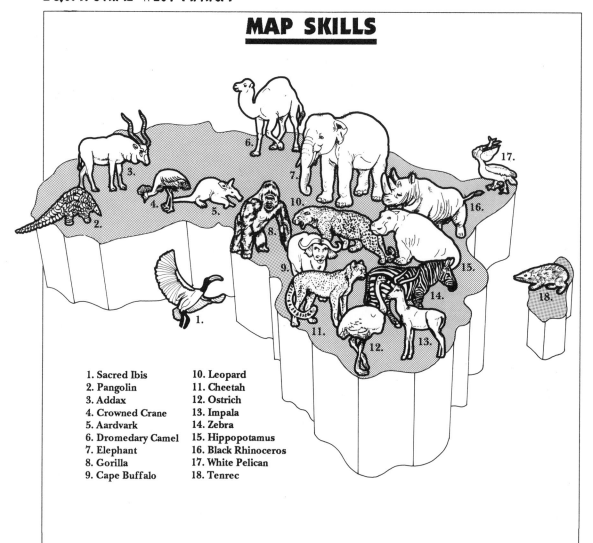

1. Sacred Ibis
2. Pangolin
3. Addax
4. Crowned Crane
5. Aardvark
6. Dromedary Camel
7. Elephant
8. Gorilla
9. Cape Buffalo
10. Leopard
11. Cheetah
12. Ostrich
13. Impala
14. Zebra
15. Hippopotamus
16. Black Rhinoceros
17. White Pelican
18. Tenrec

WILDLIFE IN AFRICA

Note: To help you answer these questions, refer to the map skills page in chapter 5.

1. In what part of Africa would you find the dromedary camel?
2. In what part of Africa does the gorilla live?
3. What animals live in the area of South Africa?
4. What animals live in the area of Zaire?
5. Name three animals pictured in the area of Uganda.
6. Name three types of birds shown to be living in Africa.

CHAPTER 3 REVIEW

Summary of Equatorial West Africa

Equatorial West Africa is a land of interesting and different types of peoples. It is a land of hot, humid rain forests and pleasant, moderately warm mountainous regions. This area is also the home to many, many different kinds of animals.

For the most part, life is hard for the people of Equatorial West Africa. Little rainfall in some regions, bitter fueds among ethnic groups in others, and poor soil in still other areas make life difficult. However, the tradition of family thrives in this part of the world just as it has for centuries.

The ethnic groups of Equatorial West Africa are ancient. Their way of life has changed little in the past centuries. Farming, housing, and customs of traditional groups and families have remained unchanged even as the industrial world has become more evident and important.

Critical Thinking Skills

Directions: Give some serious thought to the questions below. Be sure to answer in complete sentences.

1. Why do the houses in this region so often have thatched roofs?
2. Explain why small farms grow food products while the larger farms in the region grow rubber trees or coffee.
3. To what types of markets might the people of this region export beautiful hardwoods such as mahogany, ebony, and cedar?
4. How might the discovery of oil in Angola change the future of that country?
5. Explain the problems that have faced the nations of this area in their search for independence and unity.

Write It!

Directions: Explain to a person in Rwanda what houses are like in the United States.

For Discussion

Directions: Discuss these questions with your class. Appoint one class member to write the ideas you discover on the board.

1. Many of the people of Gabon live in the cities. Why is this situation unusual?
2. What are some of the things that copper is used for?
3. How do you think the Zairian rain forests are different from the forests in the United States?
4. What problems might be caused in Equatorial West Africa if a dam were to be built along the Congo River?
5. How has past colonial experience affected the culture of Equatorial West Africa?

For You To Do

Directions: Make a collage of the products of Equatorial West Africa. Cut out pictures from magazines that show the products or the ways in which the products are used. To get started, try getting pictures of copper pipes, pennies, or other copper products.

SOUTH SAHARA AFRICA

Chapter 4

F
A
C
T
S

- The Nile River and the Sahara have had a major impact on the area.
- Only 3 percent of the land in Niger is used to grow crops.
- Lack of rainfall has created conditions of great hardship and famine.
- The region has an important history as a crossroads of trade.
- Temperatures in Chad and Niger often reach as high as 120 degrees.

PART 1:
Sudan—The Nile and Desert

Sudan is the largest country in the *continent* of Africa. Many different geographical features are found in this area. Much of Sudan lies on a high *plateau*. The country includes deserts in the north, *plains* spotted with grassy wetlands, and low grass *savannas* on the central plateau. In the wetter south are the tall grass and tree savannas.

The Nile River is the key to Sudan's economy. The great river winds through this area from south to north.

Four cataracts, or waterfalls, interrupt the smooth flow of the river. Most of Sudan's 23 million people live in the Nile Valley, a vital area that contains almost all of the country's *fertile* land.

Southern Sudan receives a great deal of rainfall every year. The countryside is dense with *vegetation*. Wildlife roam freely through the savannas. Many wild animals—including gazelles, giraffes, elephants, and cats of every kind—live in the

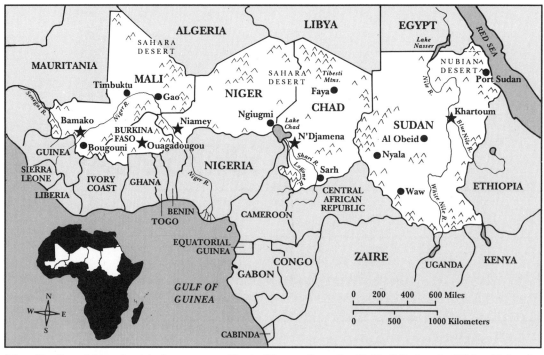

Map Study: *Approximately how many miles is Niamey from the Gulf of Guinea? With which other South Saharan countries does Chad share a border? On what river is the city of Timbuktu? In which country do you find Bamako, Gao, and Bougouni? Through which two South Saharan countries does the Niger River flow?*

south. The Nile is well known for its population of crocodiles and hippos.

Life in the Sudan

Eighty percent of the Sudanese people are engaged in agricultural activities. The country's chief crop is cotton. Sudanese cotton is famous the world over for its soft quality. Other products raised in this area are peanuts, *sorghum, millet,* and sugarcane. Sudanese farmers account for almost 85 percent of the world's gum arabic. Gum arabic comes from the acacia (uh KAY shuh) tree. The gum is used to manufacture candies and medicine.

Sudan's economy is improving. Modern irrigation projects use water from the Nile River to cultivate more land and increase farm production. Using up-to-date technology has allowed the people of the Sudan to develop small deposits of oil, iron ore, gold, copper, chromium, and mica.

The political, economic, and social center of the Sudan is Khartoum (kahr TOOM). This city is located at the junction of the Blue and White Nile. Khartoum is a city of modern architecture and dress contrasting with local traditional architecture and customs. Sudan's other important cities include Omdurman, across the Nile from Khartoum, and Port Sudan on the Red Sea.

Sugarcane is among the crops grown by Sudanese farmers.

Like other countries along the southern edge of the Sahara, Sudan has been influenced by both Arab and African *cultures*. The Nubian people and the Arabs of the north are Islamic and have a long history of contact with Egypt and the Middle East. The African Christians of the south have been strongly influenced by European missionaries.

After gaining independence in 1956, the government of Sudan tried to force the Islamic faith as well as Arabic customs on the people of the south. Since 1980 the southern region has been in rebellion against the Sudanese central government in Khartoum.

Greetings from Sudan

Hospitality is a Sudanese custom. The northern Sudanese are a formal and traditional people. However, they are very friendly in the way that they greet friends as well as strangers.

When you meet someone from Sudan, a firm but gentle handshake is usually correct. Friends often embrace. In public, men do not shake hands with, or otherwise touch, women unless the woman extends her hand first.

In northern Sudan, Arabic is widely spoken. You can expect to be greeted with "Salaam Alaykum" (Peace be upon you) or "Ahlan Wa-sahlan" (Welcome). You might also hear "Kayf Haalak?" (How are you?).

The Dinka of Sudan

The Dinka are a large *ethnic group* including about twenty-five different major subdivisions. In all, there are about one million Dinka living across the country of Sudan. The Dinka are a tall, thin people who live very simple lives.

Some Dinka are farmers. Usually, it is the elderly, the women, and the children who tend the farms. The more able-bodied men are herders. A man's cattle is the focus of most of his activities. Like other herders that we have met in these regions, the Dinka believe that a man's wealth is measured by how many cattle he owns.

According to Dinka traditions, cattle are more than just a symbol of wealth. They also have social and religious significance. The Dinka see a likeness in the lives of cattle and in their own lives. Cattle, to a Dinka herder, have rights of their own. They must never be killed for an unimportant reason. Thus, cattle are not killed to provide food. Sometimes cattle are sacrificed at religious ceremonies, but this act is considered an honor for the cow.

The Dinka have a keen sense of loyalty to their ethnic group. Although men often take more than one wife, no jealousy exists between wives. Instead, the wives live near each other and take turns in cooking and caring for their husband.

The Dinka are very concerned with agriculture, in particular with cattle-rearing on the available pasture lands. In recent years, the government of Sudan has introduced new crops for the farmers to grow in order to increase their income.

R E V I E W

Directions:
Write the reasons for the following statements. Use complete sentences.
1. Farms in the Sudan are located near the Nile River.
2. Southern Sudan has rich vegetation.
3. Khartoum is the most important city in Sudan.
4. Modern technology is important to the economic growth of Sudan.
5. The Dinka do not eat beef.

PART 2:
Chad—A Landlocked Nation

Chad is another large country in South Sahara Africa. However, Chad is an underdeveloped, poor country because it lacks natural resources and has no access to the sea. Less than six million people live in the entire country. The capital city of Chad is N'Djamena (en JAHM uh nuh). The official language of Chad is French, but most of the people speak Arabic in the north and a Bantu language in the south.

The northern part of Chad lies in the Sahara Desert and is very dry. The few people who live here are Arabs or Toubou. The Toubou are an African ethnic group. The Toubou and the Arabs make their living as herders of camels, goats, cattle, and sheep.

In the south of Chad, a large number of different African ethnic groups can be found. Many of the groups are *Bantu*. The largest group, called the Sara, are farmers. They raise crops like millet, rice, sorghum, or *cassava*. Larger farms in Southern Chad grow cotton.

Slowly, as the desert gives way, the land becomes rich with vegetation. In the far southern part of Chad, tropical forests can be found. Wild animals—including lions, elephants, giraffes, and antelope—can be seen near the forests.

A large part of Chad is a wildlife *preserve*. This vast area is called the Zakouma National Park.

Several years of drought in South Sahara Africa have destroyed many fertile and prosperous cotton fields.

The Future Outlook

As poor as Chad is today, things look worse for the future. The country is currently suffering through a severe *drought*. This drought has lasted more than ten years. Lake Chad, once a huge *lake* in the middle of the country, has been reduced to about one-tenth of its original size.

Large areas of once fertile land have become dried up and useless. Water and feed for livestock are becoming extremely difficult to find. Many Chadians have left the country in search of a better life. Other people have stayed. Some Chadians, unfortunately, have died of malnutrition and starvation.

R
E
V
I
E
W

Directions:
Use information from the text to complete each of the following sentences.
1. A large part of North Chad lies in the _____.
2. An important product of farms in South Chad is _____.
3. A long period of little or no rain is called a _____.
4. One important reason why Chad is an underdeveloped country is _____.
5. The Toubou people and the Arabs make a living by _____.

PART 3:
Burkina Faso (Upper Volta)

Burkina Faso (buur KEE nuh FAH soh) lies between Mali and Niger to the north and the Ivory Coast to the south. Cattle raising is the traditional occupation. However, drought has reduced the number of cattle by 70 percent. Sleeping sickness (which is spread by the *tsetse* fly), *famine,* and other diseases have left one-third of the country without people.

Burkina Faso was once called Upper Volta by the French. The word "burkina" means "land of honest men." "Faso" means "democratic and republican." Nevertheless the country is run by a corrupt military dictatorship.

Most of the 7 million people of Burkina Faso live in the few healthy and fertile areas of the south. These people earn a living as *subsistence* farmers. The main food crops include corn, rice, and sorghum. In addition, the country *exports* small

---

Weather in the Sahel

When a farmer lives near a great desert like the Sahara, he must always be mindful of the weather. Some years there might be a drought. Drought in this area of the world may mean NO rain for an entire year.

Another problem can be sandstorms. During the dry season, terrible winds called *haboobs* sometimes blow across the land. These storms blow dust and sand through the air. When they blow, the sky becomes a thick cloud and everything is covered with sand and dust.

The haboobs also carry things away. They carry huts, fences, and—most importantly—the fertile topsoil.

The haboobs blow dust and sand fiercely across the land.

amounts of peanuts and sesame seeds. Small manufacturing plants process farm products and building materials.

Members of 50 African ethnic groups live in the country of Burkina Faso. The largest ethnic groups include the Mande, the Gurunsi, and the Bobo.

Seasonal rains force herders to be forever on the move in a search for water. Without water, cattle die. Wells such as this one draw herds of cattle, goats, and other livestock from all over.

R E V I E W

Directions:
Use the glossary in the back of the book. Write the word that is described in each of the following definitions.
1. The cause of sleeping sickness has been traced to this insect
2. Many people die because of a lack of food in an area
3. Land which has rich soil and is capable of growing crops
4. Farmers who live and work at a level of basic existence
5. People sharing common racial, cultural, or language traditions

PART 4:
Niger—Nomads, Farmers, and Craftsmen

Niger (NY jur) is another large country jutting into the middle of Africa. Its northern areas are in the Sahara Desert and support little, if any, life. Daytime temperatures in this region *exceed* 120 degrees. There is very little rainfall.

In the far southwest of this country is the Niger River. It is from this river that the country takes its name. The Niger River travels through this area for almost 200 miles. Most Nigerians live along the river banks.

The Hausa in Niger

The capital city, Niamey (nee AHM ay), is located on the Niger River in the southwest. It is a large city of almost 400,000 people. The official language of Niger is French. However, Bantu *dialects* are spoken throughout the country.

The people of Niger belong to many different ethnic groups. The largest of these groups is the Hausa. These African ethnic groups make up about one-half the population of Niger. The Hausa are mostly farmers. They raise grains such as rice, millet, and sorghum.

Other groups include the Fulani and the Taureg. These people live in Niger only a few months of the year. During the dry season, these *nomads* go south across the border into Nigeria.

In all of Africa, those people who live along the many rivers depend upon fishing to stay alive.

As in other parts of Africa, the people of this area are noted for their art. Nigerians are famed *goldsmiths* and tinsmiths. Craftsmen also work in leather and wood.

The people of Niger are particularly proud of their culture, which blends African ethnic tradition with *Islam*.

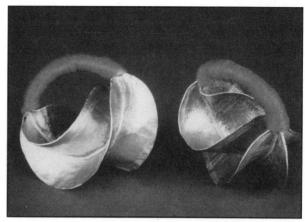

Africa has long been a source of gold to the rest of the world. As these earrings show, Nigerian craftsmen have achieved technical perfection in creating works of art.

R E V I E W

Directions:
Of the four terms listed, *one* does not belong. Can you spot the one term that does not belong? Write it on your paper.
1. Rice, millet, corn, sorghum
2. Hausa, Dinka, Fulani, Tuareg
3. Goldsmiths, herders, farmers, dentists
4. Sahara Desert, Nile River, Niger River, Niamey
5. Niger, Chad, Sudan, Angola

PART 5:
Mali—Desert and Savanna

Mali (MAHL ee) sometimes seems to be two countries. The northern two-thirds lies in the Sahara Desert and Northern Sahel. The people of this region are nomads who herd sheep, goats, camels, donkeys, and horses.

However, most of the people of Mali live in the southern region, which is made up of grass savanna plains. Farmers in the south raise corn (maize) and sorghum for food. Small amounts of peanuts and cotton are raised for export.

Increasing irrigation from the Niger River is Mali's hope for the future. Numerous foreign aid projects are building dams and irrigation channels.

In Mali, the family is the basic unit of society. As in most of Africa, the family is made up of all the descendants of a common ancestor. This means that uncles, aunts, grandparents, and cousins are important to every member of the society. The oldest male member of any family serves as the head of that group.

The family also consists of the spirits of all of the deceased members of that family. These spirits, it is believed, guide the living in every act of their lives.

At one time Malinese society included nobles, freemen, servants, and slaves. Today, all citizens are considered free and equal. The only distinction between peoples is in the type of work that they do.

Farmers, or tillers of the soil, are considered to be the noblest of all people. This feeling occurs because farming implies a type of partnership with nature. Fishermen, hunters, and cattle raisers are considered slightly less important than farmers.

In Mali, the Sahara is slowly claiming more and more farmland and forests. In some cases, an increased demand for firewood, overgrazing, and farming have forced people to relocate.

Further down the ladder of importance are the people who work as priests or traders. Though religious leaders are respected in Mali, their lives are considered less important than those who make their living by farming or fishing.

The lowest step among groups of people include artists and craftsmen. Into this *caste* fall people such as singers, musicians, historians, and storytellers or *griots*.

Because farmers are considered the noblest of people, you might suppose that these most respected members of the Malinese people actually own land. In fact, in Mali a person does not own land in the same way in which land is owned in the United States. A family may own only those things produced on the land. For example, a farmer may own the corn he grows but not the land on which it grew. No human produced the soil; therefore, no human can own it.

The actual owner of any piece of land can only use that property for producing crops or goods for the people of his village. Everyone in the village must benefit from the land. The owner is forbidden by law to destroy or sell even the smallest part of it.

R E V I E W

Directions:
Number your paper from 1-5. Then answer the following questions in complete sentences.
1. Why could Mali be considered two countries?
2. Why are farmers considered important in the Malinese society?
3. Why does traditional and modern law in Mali prevent ownership of the land?
4. How is the family organized in Malinese society?
5. Why is a belief in spirits important to the Malinese people?

SPOTLIGHT
S T O R Y

Education in South Sahara Africa

The education of the people of South Sahara Africa has been a three-step process. Many hundreds of years ago, education meant only teaching boys and girls what they needed to know to be members of the community. Boys learned hunting, farming, and cattle herding. Girls were taught to cook, to make medicines, and to raise babies.

As the Arabs came from the north, they tried to convert the natives to become *Muslims*. They brought teachers, called *marabouts*, to the area. These marabouts were responsible for educating the Africans about Islam.

After World War I, Western churches sent missionaries to South Sahara Africa. The Protestants and the Catholics attempted to convert the Africans to their religions. These missionaries taught the people how to read and write.

Today, only ten or fifteen percent of the citizens are able to read or write. Why? There are many reasons. One reason is that so many of the children of Sudan, Chad,

Education in South Sahara Africa is difficult to come by. Only ten to fifteen percent of the citizens in this region can read and write.

Mali, and other countries are nomads. The government has not yet found a way to set up schools for these wanderers. Another reason is expense. Education costs a lot of money. These countries are very poor—among the poorest in the world.

A third reason is that the children are needed at home and are not allowed by their parents to attend school. Boys are needed to tend the fields or to help with the herds. Girls are needed to help with household chores and with younger children.

A fourth reason is that religious and traditional beliefs teach the people of this area that girls should not be educated. Many Africans believe that girls should stay at home and prepare to grow up to be wives.

Education in this part of the world is of great importance. For many reasons, however, the children of the countries of South Sahara Africa are among the most *illiterate* people in the world.

Directions:

Use complete sentences to answer these questions about education in South Sahara Africa.

1. Before the Arabs came to this area, what things did the natives teach their children?
2. What things did the Arab teachers consider important for the Africans to learn?
3. What were the Arab teachers called?
4. What two Western religions sent missionaries to this area?
5. List four reasons why education is so difficult in this part of the world.

MAP SKILLS

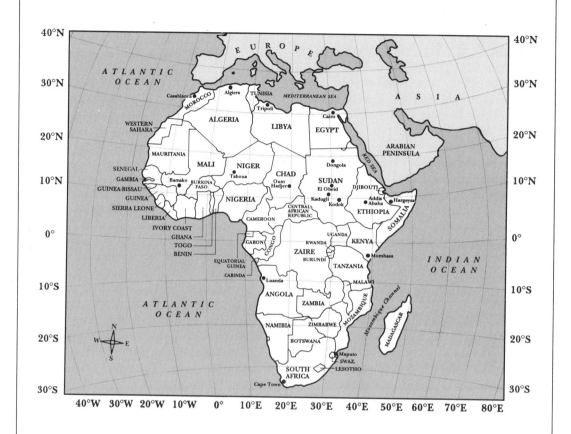

LONGITUDE AND LATITUDE
IN SOUTH SAHARA AFRICA

1. On what degree of longitude will you find the city of Oum Hadjer in Chad?
2. Near what degree of latitude will you find the city of Kodok in Sudan?
3. What city in Niger lies at approximately 15° north latitude and 5° east longitude?
4. Through which two South Sahara countries does the Prime Meridian (0° longitude) pass?

5. Which South Sahara country has a southern border that extends to within five degrees north of the equator?
6. Which Sudanese city lies at approximately 30° east longitude?

CHAPTER 4 REVIEW

Summary of South Sahara Africa

The area of Africa called South Sahara Africa is dominated by the great Sahara Desert. The desert does not stay in one place. As it moves, drought and hard times follow. Even in the areas where drought has not struck, life can be difficult. Making a living and raising a family in this part of the world are never easy. Still, many people make South Sahara Africa their home. They live as farmers, herders, and artisans. The people of this region are noted goldsmiths and tinsmiths.

Critical Thinking Skills

Directions: Give some serious thought to the questions below. Be sure to answer in complete sentences.

1. Why do you think Khartoum, the capital city of Sudan, is located at the meeting point of two rivers?
2. How do you think the farmers in this region survive in years of drought?
3. What would you do if you lived in Burkina Faso and were unable to feed your family?
4. Why do you think the Chadian government provides a national park to protect wildlife?

Write It!

Imagine that you are a farmer in northern Mali. For the past fifteen years, the drought has persisted and the land has become drier and drier. How would you describe your situation to an American farmer in Iowa?

For Discussion:

Directions: Discuss these questions with your class. Appoint one class member to write ideas you discover on the board.

1. If rainfall is so scarce in South Sahara Africa, why don't the people move elsewhere?
2. Why might a Dinka wish to become a "master of the fishing spear"? How is this desire good for the ethnic group?
3. What part of a nomad's life seems to be desirable? What part seems to be undesirable?
4. What are some reasons for growing acacia trees?
5. What are some reasons that people in this area are not able to read and write?

For You To Do:

Directions: Visit a library and read about the Native Americans. They, too, were often nomads. However, various groups traveled from place to place for different reasons. Find out why many groups of Native Americans were nomadic.

SOUTHERN AFRICA

Chapter 5

F
A
C
T
S

- The vast Okavango swamps in Botswana are full of exotic wildlife.
- Southern Africa is a storehouse of minerals, gold, and diamonds.
- In Swaziland, the king's mother is in charge of national rituals.
- Zimbabwe contains ruins of an ancient city built over 500 years ago.
- Apartheid is a problem that has worldwide significance.

PART 1:
The Republic of South Africa

Southern Africa is a land dominated by the presence of the Republic of South Africa. South Africa is different from many of the countries that we have studied in this book. The most noticeable difference is that it is governed by whites and is based on white supremacy. It is the only country in Africa whose government is run by people of European descent. In addition, unlike many other African countries, South Africa is very wealthy. Even though South Africa dominates

this area, you can't ignore the history of Zimbabwe, the wildlife of Malawi, and the proud peoples of the other countries of this area.

South Africa: The Wealthiest Nation on the Continent

The Republic of South Africa is a country located at the very southern end of Africa. It is one of the most remarkable countries in all the world. Its land area covers about 4 percent of the African *continent*. Only about

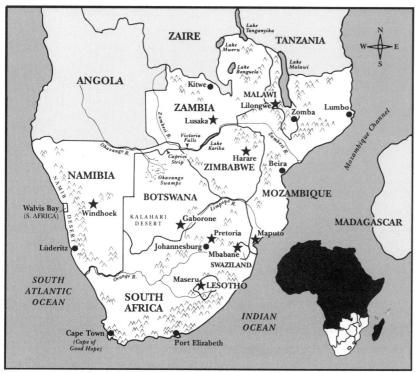

Map Study: *Which Southern African countries border the Indian Ocean? What Southern African country borders Angola, Zaire, and Tanzania? In what country do you find Capetown, the Cape of Good Hope, and the Limpopo River? Between which two countries is Victoria Falls? In which country do you find the Okavango Swamps, the Caprivi strip, and the Okavango River?*

amount of gold and diamonds of any country in the world. It is also the leading African producer of automobiles, electricity, machinery, and many other goods.

The Geography of South Africa

The Republic of South Africa lies at the southern end of the African continent. It is made up of four provinces (Cape, Natal, Transvaal, and Orange Free State). It is the only country in Africa that lies almost entirely in the region that is called the Temperate Zone (Middle Latitudes—22 degrees south to 35 degrees south.)

Except for a narrow, *coastal plain,* the country is mainly a great *plateau.* The western and northern parts of the plateau are desert. The rest is a grassy prairie land, known as a veld. The highveld is a large area of high plains and *grasslands* located in the east central interior. The bushveld

6 percent of the people of Africa live in the Republic of South Africa. Yet the Republic of South Africa produces 40 percent of the manufactured goods of Africa, 50 percent of its minerals, and 20 percent of all its farm products.

In short, the Republic of South Africa is by far the wealthiest nation in all of Africa. It produces the largest is a *savanna* of short trees and bushes at lower levels. The lowveld includes a dry, tall tree savanna and the moist forest found near the coastal plain.

The Peoples of South Africa

South Africa contains an interesting mixture of people. It is a country of nearly 37 million people divided into four categories by the government.

One group is Asians. About 2 million of them live in South Africa. Most came from India to work on huge sugarcane *plantations.*

Approximately 26 million black South Africans also live in South Africa. Many are descendants of *Bantu ethnic groups* such as the Zulu and the Xhosa. Others are from the the Sotho and Tswana ethnic groups.

Almost 3 million people of mixed race form a third group in South Africa. These people are a mix of black African, white, or Asian races.

A fourth group in South Africa is the whites. Of the 5 million or so white people in South Africa, most are *Afrikaners* (af ri KAHN urz). This term applies to the descendants of the Dutch, Germans, and French who settled in South Africa in the 17th and 18th centuries. Other whites came from England, Ireland, and Scotland in the 19th century.

History of European Settlement

For almost 1000 years before the arrival of the Dutch in 1652, groups of Africans had been migrating into the area. These people are known as Bantu-speaking peoples because they spoke languages that were similar. However, their cultures and histories were very different. Non-Bantu groups, such as the Khoi and Huttentots, also lived in the area.

The Zulu were one of these Bantu groups who migrated to South Africa. By the early 19th century, Zulu King Shaka had built a strong military empire. He developed new methods of warfare and reorganized his army into a powerful fighting force. He successfully expanded the Zulu empire into much of modern day South Africa.

The building of this empire resulted in many changes. The peoples defeated by the Zulu left their traditional homelands and moved north, forcing still other peoples farther north.

At about the same time, fateful events were taking place to the south of the Zulu empire. In 1652 the Dutch East India Company sent colonists to the southern tip of South Africa. The colonists were to grow vegetables and raise cattle to be sold to the ships traveling between Europe and India and the East Indies. The Cape Colony, as it was called, became very successful.

The Dutch settlers were known as *Boers,* which in Dutch means "farmers." They are the ancestors of about 70 percent of modern white South Africans, who are today known as Afrikaners. The Boer language is called *Afrikaans* (af ri KAHNZ), which is made up of the African, old Dutch, and Malay languages.

In the early 1800s, the British took control of the Cape Colony and its main city, Cape Town. The Boers disliked the English, and they showed their resentment by leaving. Loading all of their belongings along with their families into wagons, they set out for land north of the Cape. It was at this time that the European Boers came into contact with the expanding Zulu empire and the migrating Bantu-speaking peoples.

When the Boers began their Great Trek or migration north (1835-1837), they met few native Africans. This situation was due to the Zulu expansion. This area, north of the Orange River, had recently lost a large part of its population. Wars had killed many people, some were hiding, and still others had moved because of normal nomadic custom.

The Boers set up two independent countries—the Orange Free State and the Transvaal. At the same time (1843), the English established the colony of Natal on the Indian Ocean Coast.

The Boers soon came into conflict with the Zulu and fought for over 40 years for control of the land. Neither was able to win a controlling victory.

In 1868 diamonds were found near Kimberly in the Orange Free State. Later, the world's largest gold deposits were found near Johannesburg in the Transvaal. The discovery of these gold deposits brought a large number of English settlers to the Boer Republics. In 1879 the British became involved in the Boer-Zulu wars. The Zulu defeated the British in several battles, but superior weapons and manpower eventually led to the British destruction of the Zulu empire. At the same time, the British defeated the Xhosa and the Tswana, two other ethnic peoples of South Africa.

The discovery of diamonds and gold brought thousands of British, while other Europeans also invaded the area. In 1899 hostile feelings between the British and the Boers broke out in the South African War, also called the Boer War. The Boers used guerilla warfare, and the British set up concentration camps in which many Boer civilians died. This bitter war continued for three years. Finally, in 1902, the Boers surrendered.

In 1910 the British created the Union of South Africa. A Boer leader was named as the chief administrator to ensure that the white Boer minority would maintain control. During the next four decades, an unofficial policy of racial separateness existed.

In the 1948 elections, the government of South Africa came under the control of the extremist nationalist party that has controlled it ever since. The nationalist party's goals have been to set up, by law, the separation of the races. This goal has been accomplished through a policy of "separate development" or *apartheid.*

The idea of "separate development" is that each race, apart from other races, is to improve its own culture and future. However, the apartheid laws have been used to reinforce Boer (Afrikaner) privilege status, power, and wealth.

Apartheid Grips South Africa

Apartheid has brought international attention to South Africa. Although whites make up less than 15 percent of the population, they control the government. Black South Africans, Asians, and people of mixed race are not allowed to participate in the government to any significant, contributing degree.

Apartheid means "separateness" in Afrikaan, one of South Africa's official languages. In reality, it means *discrimination* against all non-white people. It means that black South Africans, Asians, and people of mixed race are not allowed to live in the same areas as whites, send their children to the same schools, or even swim on the same beaches.

In 1912 four young lawyers, all black, formed the South African Native National Congress. The purpose of this political party was to unite all the blacks of South Africa in an effort to protest the injustices. This party later became the African National Congress (ANC).

Apartheid became an official government policy in 1948. It has been in effect ever since. In fact, until the 1980s, an official government identification card was needed by all non-whites to enter a white neighborhood.

This system of apartheid has been universally condemned by almost every other nation in the world. South Africa has been cut off from the rest of the world by *sanctions*. Some countries have refused to trade with South Africa and refused to recognize their government. Such sanctions can hurt the country economically.

Nelson Mandela

One of the leaders of the ANC, Nelson Mandela, is a particularly important man. Mandela was a leader in the ANC when the movement was gaining in popularity.

In 1956 Mandela was arrested and charged wth high treason. In 1961 Mandela was acquitted, or found not guilty, of the charges.

Archbishop Tutu dances along with other residents of the black township, Soweto, following the announcement that jailed ANC leader, Nelson Mandela, will be freed.

South Africa's State President, F. W. DeKlerk, poses with the leader of the African National Congress, Nelson Mandela, upon Mandela's release from prison.

Later, in 1961, the police once again sought to arrest Mandela for organizing black protests against the policies of the South African government. Mandela was arrested again in August of 1962 and was imprisoned in a fort in Johannesburg. This time he was found guilty of inciting the people to strike and for leaving the country without documents. He was sentenced to five years in prison.

Mandela was not defeated. He continued to be a leader of his people even from prison. The government of South Africa moved to silence Mandela and in 1963 convicted him of high treason. Mandela was sentenced to life in prison.

SPOTLIGHT
S T O R Y

Mandela's Commitment to End Apartheid

For Nelson Mandela, life in prison meant that he would now have to continue his struggles from a jail cell. The following speech explains the frustrations and feelings of those who live under the law of apartheid.

"Africans want to be paid a living wage. Africans want to perform work which they are capable of doing and not work which the government declares them capable of. Africans want to live where they obtain work and not to be chased out of an area because they were not born there. Africans want to own land in places where they work and not be obliged to live in rented houses which they can never call their own. We want to be part of the general population and not confined to living in ghettoes.

African Congress Leader, Nelson Mandela, and his wife, Winnie, raise fists following his release from Victor Vester prison on February 27, 1990, after 27 years in captivity.

African men want to have their wives and children to live with them where they work and not be forced into an unnatural existence in men's hostels. African women want to be with their menfolk and not be left permanently widowed in the reserves. We want to travel in our own country and seek work where we want and not where the Labor Bureau tells us to.

We want a just share of the whole of South Africa; we want security and a stake in society.

Above all, we want equal political rights because without them our disabilities will be permanent. I know this sounds revolutionary to the whites of this country because the majority of voters will be Africans. This makes the white man fear democracy. But this fear cannot be allowed to stand in the way of the only solution which will guarantee racial harmony and freedom for all..."

Stop and Review
1. What is the meaning of the term "frustration" as it is used in this reading?
2. What are some of the economic desires of the black peoples of South Africa?
3. What are some of the civil rights that Nelson Mandela demands for the people of South Africa?
4. Why are Afrikaners afraid to grant complete equality of civil rights to the Africans of South Africa?
5. If you were a black South African, how would you feel about Mandela's ideas?

The land in the homelands is often very poor, and the people are barely able to survive.

Mandela's story did not end in 1963. Twenty-seven years later, Mandela still serves as a leader in the ANC. In 1990, at the age of 71, Mandela was finally released from prison by F. W. DeKlerk, the president of South Africa. Upon his release, Mandela still proclaimed his dedication to the struggle of the blacks of South Africa. "Our march to freedom is irreversible," he said. "We must not allow fear to stand in our way."

Today, the struggle against apartheid continues; and Nelson Mandela, as a member of the African National Congress, still leads that struggle.

Mongosuthu Buthelezi is a prince of the "Zulu nation." He is currently the president of Inkhata, the Zulu political and cultural movement. While Nelson Mandela was in prison, Buthelezi became the chief minister of KwaZulu, one of the ten homelands set up by the Afrikaners. As a result, Buthelezi has been accused of supporting apartheid.

In answer to this charge, Buthelezi has made repeated calls for compromise with the white minority. His pioneer program—"Natal-KwaZulu Indaba," a formula for black-white power-sharing in local government, could be attempted on a national scale.

Homelands and Townships

South Africa's government has created special territories, called *homelands*, where blacks must live. According to the white government, these areas are supposed to allow black South Africans to develop their own nations. Unfortunately, they are a way to maintain white domination and privilege.

Minerals, natural resources, and good soil for growing crops are reserved for places where whites live. Homelands are usually the poorest, least desirable land. Often they are in the mountains or the deserts. Poverty and hunger are widespread.

Only about half of all black South Africans live within their homelands. The others live in the *townships* or near the mines and factories in which they work.

Townships are black sections connected to or located near a white city. The black South Africans who are allowed to live in the township must work in the connected city. The townships are filled with poverty and hunger.

Soweto, outside of Johannesburg, is the largest of all the townships; it has over one million citizens.

Winnie Mandela, representing the people of the Alexandra township, talks to a senior police officer about their grievances on living conditions during a rally.

Ways of Life

When we look at the way in which South Africans live, we will need to look at each group differently. The whites of South Africa are chiefly an *urban* group. Their homes, dress, and foods are much like you would expect to see in any American city. One difference is that many whites in this country employ black South Africans as servants. Such help exists because so much cheap labor is available.

Most Asians and people of mixed race live in the cities of South Africa. The majority of both of these groups work in low paying jobs. Many are servants, factory workers, or plantation workers.

Work is scarce for many of the blacks in South Africa. Most blacks are unskilled laborers and must travel to find work. Their families are rarely permitted to go with them.

R E V I E W

Directions:
Choose from the list of words to complete the sentences. Write the complete sentence on your paper.

apartheid   Zulu   Boers   townships   Xhosa   homelands

1. Dutch settlers were known as _____, which means "farmers."
2. Black sections connected to white cities are called _____.
3. Special territories created for blacks to live in are called _____.
4. Two large ethnic groups living in South Africa are the _____ and the _____.
5. The system of race relations in South Africa is called _____.

SPOTLIGHT
S T O R Y

The Zulu

Without a doubt, the most widely known ethnic group in all of Africa is the Zulu. The Zulu are a Bantu people. Members of this group live mainly in South Africa. About half of the Zulu in South Africa live in a township called KwaZulu. Sometimes this area is referred to as Zululand.

The Zulu people are famous because they have a tradition of being fierce warriors. This reputation came to the Zulu under the rule of a king called Shaka. Shaka was the son of a Zulu chief. At a young age, his mother took him from his village to be raised by the Mthetwa. The Mthetwa were a warlike people.

Soon Shaka grew to be a capable warrior and leader. Living with the Mthetwa, he became a leader in the army. When Shaka's father died, Shaka returned to the Zulu and took command of them by force.

Under Shaka's rule, the Zulu nation expanded. He trained thousands of warriors and molded them into an *invincible* army. Shaka devised new battle *tactics* and invented new weapons. He proved to the Zulu warriors that the throwing spear that they used was useless. Instead, he commanded his armies to carry short spears used for stabbing. Shaka was a military genius.

Shaka was murdered by his own brothers in 1828. He had ruled the Zulu for twelve years. During that time, he had become a cruel and hated ruler. However, he also had become the leader of a great and powerful nation. Fifty years after Shaka's death, the Zulu was still the largest and fiercest nation of black Africans.

As the British moved to expand their influence over the area of Zululand, they met with tremendous resistance. In 1872 an enormous British army was sent out to capture the Zulu chief and crush his armies. Only 55 British soldiers survived. The Zulu engaged the British in close fighting. They used their stabbing spears to completely crush the British army. The methods of warfare devised by Shaka over fifty years before brought about a massive defeat for the British soldiers. However, in further battles, the guns and cannons of the British overcame the spears and shields of the Zulu. The chief was captured, and the Zulu army was soundly defeated.

The Zulu nation was confined to Zululand and governed first by the British and then by the South Africans. Today, the Zulu ethnic group suffers under the hardships of apartheid. Still, these proud people hold on to their traditions and their customs.

Stop and Review
Directions: Answer the following questions about the Zulu.
1. What weapon did Shaka introduce to the Zulu warriors?
2. From where did the original Zulu come?
3. Where do most of the Zulu people live today?
4. What group in the history of the United States reminds you of the Zulu experience in Africa?
5. What army eventually defeated the Zulu?

PART 2:
Namibia—The Road to Independence

Namibia (nuh MIB ee uh) is located along the Atlantic coast to the west and north of South Africa. Before 1919 Namibia was a German colony, German Southwest Africa. During World War I (1914-1918), soldiers from the Union of South Africa drove out the Germans. Since then, South Africa has ruled the area.

Namibia is a very dry country. Along the coast is the Namib desert. The name Namibia means "land of the Namib." Farther east and inland is the Kalahari Desert. Most of the people live in the highlands of Central Namibia where the climate is cooler and not as dry.

The peoples of Namibia—both black and white—earn their living through ranching and cattle and sheep raising on the savanna and in the highlands. Fishing along the Atlantic Coast is also an important source of income. However, the greatest sources of jobs are Namibia's mineral resources. Along the coast in the south are large diamond deposits. In the savanna and uplands, large deposits of uranium, copper, lead, and zinc are mined.

Apartheid was introduced into Namibia at the same time that it was introduced into South Africa. As a result, even though 90 percent of the population is black, the government and wealth has been controlled by Afrikaners and other whites from South Africa. A legislature, which does have black representation, has been controlled by whites through racial allotments.

Beginning in the late 1970s, Namibian black rebel groups began fighting for the independence of the area. The rebels attacked South African troops from bases in Angola. South African troops, in turn, attacked rebel bases that were inside South Angola. Discussions between the rebels and representatives of South Africa took place throughout the 1980s. In 1988 an agreement was reached in regard to independence for Namibia. In November of 1989, an assembly was elected to write a constitution for the new country. Finally, on December 22, 1989, a final agreement was signed at the United Nations, granting Namibia its independence.

R
E
V
I
E
W

Directions:
Number your paper from 1 to 5. Write the word *true* if the statement is true. Write the word *false* if the statement is false.
1. Few, if any, mineral resources exist in Namibia.
2. The Namib and Kalahari Deserts are important parts of Namibia's topography.
3. Apartheid was never introduced into Namibia.
4. Blacks in Namibia have participated in government on a limited basis.
5. The Namibians have been unsuccessful in their struggle for independence.

PART 3:
Swaziland, Botswana, Lesotho

Swaziland (SWAHZ ee land) is a beautiful country surrounded on three sides by South Africa. Its neighbor to the northeast is Mozambique. It is a land of rich, *fertile* soil and has many natural resources and minerals. Large forests dot the countryside, and picturesque mountains accent the land.

Despite all of its riches, the people of Swaziland are mostly *peasant* farmers. This situation exists because almost half of the land in Swaziland is owned by outsiders, mainly South Africans and white Europeans.

The Swazi of Swaziland

Almost all (90 percent) of the people of Swaziland are black. Of these people, 95 percent are from an ethnic group called the Swazi—a people of Bantu origin. The Swazi are noted for their highly developed warrior system. They were once regarded as fierce enemies by others in the region. This factor has made Swaziland a unified country. The Swazis have a common language and traditions. The rules of law and government are based on Swazi traditional customs.

The Swazi regard cattle as valuable property. In fact, when a Swazi man marries, he must pay his bride's family in cattle. A man's wealth in Swaziland is often measured by how many cattle he owns. A farmer with a large herd is respected by other men, yet cattle are rarely slaughtered and used for food. Instead, they are traded or sold for cash. The Swazi also use cattle for religious ceremonies.

In addition to raising cattle, Swazi farmers grow a number of crops. A

Swazi farm might include fields of *cassava,* rice, or corn. Larger farms are usually owned by South Africans. These plantations grow crops to export. These crops include pineapples, sugarcane, and tobacco. An unusual crop in Swaziland is the *eucalyptus* tree. Plantation owners have planted eucalyptus forests in the mountainous areas of Swaziland. These wooded areas are among the largest man-made forests in Africa.

Heavy machinery is not found in most farming areas in Southern Africa. Farmers work their land as their ancestors did—with oxen and a plow.

Farms, mines, and businesses in South Africa employ about one-third of Swaziland's workers. Most workers spend at least six months a year working in South Africa. The rest of the labor force works in small, local mining and lumbering operations. Swaziland is fortunate in having mineral resources: gold, coal, asbestos, iron, and lumber.

Unlike Lesotho, only about 20 percent of Swaziland's trade is with South Africa. It also has access to the sea through part of Maputo in neighboring Mozambique.

Mbabane: Capital of Swaziland

The capital city of Swaziland is Mbabane (em buh BAHN). In Swazi towns and cities, most of the people live in houses much like you would see in an American city. In the countryside, the people usually live in huts arranged in homesteads. A homestead is a group of huts in which a single extended family might live. Since a Swazi man may have more than one wife, the homesteads are sometimes quite large.

Cattle are very important to the people of Swaziland. Men gain respect from other members of the community by the size of their herd.

SOUTHERN AFRICA

Botswana

Botswana (baht SWAHN uh) was the former British territory of Bechuanaland (bech uh WAHN uh land). Botswana lies north of South Africa between Namibia and Zimbabwe. It is an arid, *landlocked* country about the size of the state of Texas. Much of the country lies on a high plateau in the Kalahari (Kal uh HAHR ee) Desert.

The British took control of Botswana in 1866 to connect the Cape with Rhodesia (Zimbabwe and Zambia) and to avoid the Boers in the Transvaal. The British invested little in the area. At the time of independence in 1966, there were no paved roads or electricity and only one important factory, a meat-canning plant.

Today, about 75 percent of Botswana's workers farm or raise cattle. The main food products include maize (corn), *sorghum, millet,* cowpeas (black-eyed peas), and cattle. Mineral deposits of diamonds, copper, nickel, and coal provide jobs and income. Most *exports* and *imports* must come through South Africa.

About 1.2 million people live in Botswana. The major ethnic group is the Bantu-speaking Tswana (almost 95 percent of the people). This fact gives Botswana unity and national

---

Education in Lesotho

The school systems in Lesotho are very much like the school systems in Europe. In fact, Lesotho's schools are patterned after those in Great Britain.

All children may attend an elementary school for seven years. Each year is called a standard.

After completing seven standards, the children of Lesotho take an examination. If the student passes the examination and if his parents can afford tuition, secondary education can begin. After another three years and another exam, a Junior Certificate is given.

---

identity. English is the official language, but only one-fourth of the people speak it. Almost everyone speaks Tswana, a Bantu language.

Most of Botswana's people live along the wetter eastern area where a dry savanna geography exists. Within the Kalahari live the Khoi, who are nomadic hunters and gatherers.

Lesotho

Lesotho (luh SOH toh) is completely surrounded by the Republic of South Africa. Very little land is suitable for farming. However, its rugged land has prevented successful invasion. A tradition of independence prevented the kingdom from being included in South Africa.

Most of Lesotho's 1.6 million people live in small villages. More than 95 percent are members of the Ba Sotho, a Bantu group. Traditionally, the Ba Sotho live in communities arranged around a *kraal* where cattle are kept. The English word "corral" comes from the Ba Sotho kraal.

Few natural resources and a lack of level land cause many people to leave Lesothos to work in the mines of South Africa. All imported and exported products such as diamonds, wool, and food must be sent through South Africa. These factors make it very difficult for this small nation to become truly independent.

R E V I E W

Directions:
Write *Lesotho, Botswana, Swaziland,* or *All* for each statement to identify the country to which it refers.
1. Completely surrounded by the Republic of South Africa
2. Once a colony of Great Britain
3. Cattle raising is an important source of food and income.
4. An important unifying factor is its one very large ethnic group.
5. Mining provides products for export and jobs.

PART 4:
Zimbabwe, Zambia, Malawi

Zimbabwe (Zim BAHB wee) is a country that takes its name from ancient inhabitants. Over five hundred years ago, a great and powerful people, the Karanga, lived in this area. Karanga *dynasties* ruled much of the land in what is now Zimbabwe, Mozambique, and Zambia. The Karanga word for capital city was "Zimbabwe." Their largest city, the Great Zimbabwe, was located in what is now the southern part of this country. The ancient ruins are still there, a marvel and a mystery to all who visit. These ruins are a symbol of the achievements of African *cultures* before the arrival of the Europeans.

Over a hundred years ago, Zimbabwe was called Matabeleland because it was inhabited by a Bantu ethnic group called the Matabele. In the 1880s, a man named Cecil Rhodes forced the Matabele to surrender ownership of their land to the British.

Matabeleland, along with what is now called Zambia, became a country called Rhodesia. Then, at the end of the century, Rhodesia became two countries: Southern Rhodesia and Northern Rhodesia. After the Africans won a struggle with a white supremacy regime similar to South Africa's in April of 1980, Southern Rhodesia became the independent country of Zimbabwe. Northern Rhodesia became the independent country of Zambia.

The Geography of Zimbabwe

Zimbabwe is a breathtakingly beautiful country, shaped like a bowl turned upside down. The middle part of the country is a high plateau. The edges of Zimbabwe are lower lands. The country is landlocked with Mozambique to its east, Botswana to its west, Zambia to its north, and the Republic of South Africa to its south.

Zimbabwe extends from the dry savanna along the Limpopo River in the south to the tree savannas along the Zambezi River in the north. Most of this area is a highland plateau of rolling plains and hills. The climates are mild, and soils are rich.

About 80 percent of the people farm; they raise tobacco, tea, sugarcane, cotton, and corn. Zimbabwe is free of the *tsetse* fly, so herders raise cattle and sheep for meat. The country also has large deposits of copper, chromium, asbestos, and coal.

The capital of Zimbabwe is Harare. The official language in Zimbabwe is English, but most people speak one of the Bantu languages. The Matabele still live in large numbers in Zimbabwe. Sometimes the Matabele are called the Ndebele. The largest ethnic group in the country is Mashona.

Zambia: Copper is King

Zambia (ZAM bee uh), formerly Northern Rhodesia, is located north of Zimbabwe and has a similar history. It became an independent country in 1964, 15 years before Zimbabwe.

Zambia takes its name from the great Zambezi River. The magnificent, world-famous Victoria Falls is located on this river. It is one of the most spectacular sights in the world.

The capital city is Lusaka (loo SAHK uh). Once again, as in Zimbabwe, the official language is English. However, almost all Zambians are of Bantu origin and speak one of the ethnic *dialects*. The largest ethnic groups in Zambia are the Tonga, the Barotse, the Ila, and the Bemba.

Though located near the *equator*, Zambia has a mild climate. That is

Victoria Falls

In the native language, Victoria Falls is called "Mosi-oa-tunya." That name means "the smoke that thunders." During the rainy season, which lasts from March to May, over one million gallons of water drop over the falls per second! The splashing water sends a smoke-like spray hundreds of feet into the air. The deafening roar of the water sounds just like thunder!

Victoria Falls is almost one mile wide and 350 feet high. That's over twice the height and twice the width of Niagara Falls. Victoria Falls is fed by the Zambezi River system and is one of the largest *tourist* attractions in the area. At the bottom of the falls, tourist boats must share the waters with crocodiles and hippopotamuses.

Beautiful Victoria Falls can be seen along the Zambezi River.

because Zambia is mostly in an area of high *altitude*. Being up in the mountains also allows Zambians to grow many different kinds of crops.

Farming in Zambia

Farmers in Zambia live much the same as farmers in the neighboring countries. Farmers work small plots of land that are located right next to their houses. Their houses are usually simple, circular in design, and made from mud. The roofs are made of dried grass bundled together.

Zambian farmers grow corn, sorghum, cassava, and peanuts. Farmers with access to the roads and railroads grow peanuts, cotton, tobacco, and corn for export. The Zambian government is trying to improve *agriculture* in the rural areas, away from the roads and railroads, by developing cooperative farms.

The chief industry in Zambia involves copper. Copper mines have attracted many workers who, until recently, have been farmers. Growth in mining has caused the cities of Zambia to grow very quickly. As the people leave the farms, they *migrate* toward the cities that develop near the copper mining areas. Zambia also exports cobalt, lead, emeralds, uranium, and vanadium. Vanadium is a

Religion in Malawi

Approximately one-half of all Malawians follow traditional African religious beliefs. These beliefs revolve around the idea that all things—whether they be alive or dead, human or animal—are part of a vital life force. Relatives and rulers who have passed away are thought to watch over family and village affairs. These beliefs are sometimes called *animism*.

About 35 percent of all Malawians are Christians. The Christian church began sending missionaries to Malawi in the 1850s. The remaining 15 percent of the people in Malawi are *Muslims,* followers of the Islamic religion.

gray powder used to harden steel. The mining industry not only provides jobs for Zambians but also much of the government's income.

Malawi

Malawi (muh LAH wee) was once known as Nyasaland. Malawi is landlocked between Zambia to the west and Mozambique to the east. Lake Malawi fills much of the rift valley and forms most of Malawi's eastern border. Its climate is moderate even though it is near the equator because of the high altitude at which Malawi is located. This moderate climate and plentiful rainfall make conditions in Malawi ideal for farming.

Bantu peoples make up 95 percent of Malawi's population. The chief ethnic groups include the Ngoni, descended from the Zulu, and the Tonga. Malawi became independent from Great Britain in 1963. About three-quarters of the people are Christian. English and Chichewa, a traditional Bantu language, are the official languages of the country.

Malawi has about 7.5 million people. Most of them are farmers. Export crops include coffee, tobacco, tea, sugarcane, peanuts, and cotton. Crops raised for food on a local basis are corn, cassava, potatoes, and millet, along with other grains. Malawi lacks mineral resources, and even today manufacturing remains very limited.

Malawi's main problem is its location. Like all landlocked countries, Malawi depends on its neighbors for the safe passage of its imports and exports. As a result, Malawi's government has not been able to take a strong stand against South Africa.

Malawi's major resources are its wildlife; Lake Malawi; and its beautiful, forested highlands and mountains. Large game reserves have been created in many parts of the country. With new roads and hotels, Malawi could profit greatly from tourism.

R
E
V
I
E
W

Directions:
Number your paper from 1 to 6. Then, answer the following questions.
1. Why are the ruins of the Great Zimbabwe important to history?
2. Why have the people of Zimbabwe been able to raise cattle and sheep?
3. How did Zimbabwe get its name? Why was it changed?
4. Why do the people of Zambia build their huts of mud and dry grass?
5. Why is copper "king" in Zambia?
6. Why is Malawi completely dependent upon South Africa for jobs?

PART 5:
Mozambique

Mozambique (moh zum BEEK) has many harbors located on the southeast coast of Africa. It is a *tropical* country with a typical warm climate. Very little information had been available on Mozambique until about the 15th century. At that time, the Karanga, under the rule of Mwene Mutapa, ruled all of the area.

It is known that Arabs had been sailing to Mozambique for many years. The Karanga and the Arabs had developed a strong trade relationship with the area. The Arabs brought woven cloth, glass, tools, and beads to trade. In return, they traded for ivory, gold, rhinoceros horns, and slaves. The trade between the Karanga and Arabs was very successful. By the 1400s great markets existed solely for the purpose of trading with Arab sea captains.

Then, in the second half of the 15th century, Vasco da Gama set sail from Portugal and landed in

A Luta Continua!

A Luta Continua. In Portuguese, the official language of Mozambique, the phrase means "The struggle continues." The struggle began in 1962 when the people of Mozambique banded together to throw out their colonial rulers, the Portuguese.

Under the Portuguese, conditions were very bad for the people for Mozambique. Most people were not able to get proper health care, food, clothing, housing, or education. However, today, all of these things are available to all of the people.

Mozambique has only been an independent country since 1975. Great improvement has been made already. The leaders of Mozambique know that more must be done for the people. *A Luta Continua!*

Slash and burn farming is a primitive method used in African nations. The stubble is burned off after the crops have been harvested.

Mozambique. Da Gama reported back to the Portuguese that there was great wealth to be had in Mozambique. By 1629, the area of what is now Mozambique became a Portuguese *colony.*

The people of Mozambique are almost all black Africans of Bantu origin. The largest ethnic group in Mozambique is called the Makua-Lomwe.

Most of the people in Mozambique earn a living as farmers. The land is good for growing because the area is near the ocean and receives plenty of rainfall. The main obstacle to farming is the dense tropical forest that takes up much of the usable land.

Slash and Burn Farming

Farmland in this area is cleared by the "slash and burn" farming method. This method of cutting down trees and burning the remaining brush has been used for centuries. However, the method robs the soil of its nutrients and its ability to keep water. Slash and burn farming quickly tires out the soil so more and more land is needed to farm.

Mozambique has abundant natural resources for development. Good farmland covers about one-third of the land area, and water resources are plentiful. The farmers produce tea, sugarcane, cotton, cashew nuts, *sisal* (hemp), and copra (the dried meat of the coconut from which coconut oil is obtained). As more land is developed and newer farming methods are developed, other cash crops can be raised.

There are deposits of coal (which is rare in Africa), iron ore bauxite (aluminum), and asbestos. The export of these minerals adds strength to Mozambique's economy.

The Economy of Mozambique

The general economy of Mozambique is not well developed. Farming is the major source of income. Industry is limited to oil refining and food processing. Some Mozambicans earn a living catching fish and shrimp from the Indian Ocean. Many men leave their homes for months at a time to find work in South Africa.

Neighboring countries such as South Africa, Zimbabwe, Swaziland, and Malawi all use Mozambique's railways and port facilities. The country receives a fee for the usage.

R E V I E W

Directions:
Change one word in each sentence to make it true.
1. The people of Mozambique fish in the Pacific Ocean.
2. In 1629 Mozambique became a French colony.
3. Most of the people of Mozambique earn a living in mining.
4. The dried meat of the coconut is called sisal.
5. The major ethnic group of Mozambique is the Portuguese.

SOUTHERN AFRICA

MAP SKILLS

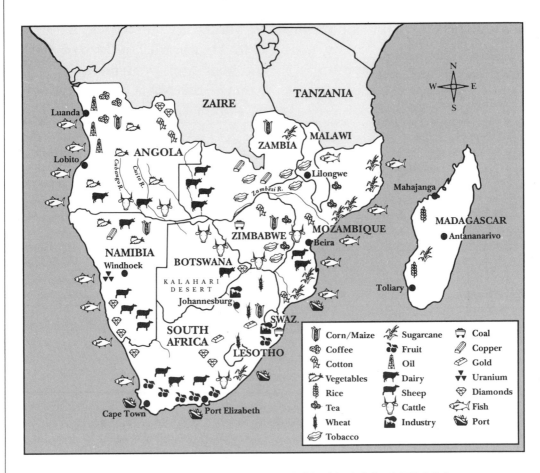

Map legend:
- Corn/Maize
- Coffee
- Cotton
- Vegetables
- Rice
- Tea
- Wheat
- Tobacco
- Sugarcane
- Fruit
- Oil
- Dairy
- Sheep
- Cattle
- Industry
- Coal
- Copper
- Gold
- Uranium
- Diamonds
- Fish
- Port

PRODUCT MAP OF SOUTHERN AFRICA

1. What product is found near Lobito in Angola as well as near Beira in Mozambique?
2. What two products can be found in Botswana near the Kalahari Desert?
3. Near what port city in South Africa might you find a lot of fruit?
4. Name four products found in Namibia.
5. In which country can you expect to find gold mines?
6. What cash crop is grown near the Zambezi River in Zambia?

CHAPTER 5 REVIEW

Summary of Southern Africa

Southern Africa is a breathtakingly beautiful land. Its towering mountain ranges, inspirational waterways, and broad plateaus make it a marvelous spot for tourists to visit. It is also a land of great potential wealth. Vast amounts of gold, diamonds, uranium, and copper are hidden in the ground. Cattle thrive in great numbers.

The history of the people of Southern Africa is rich, too. The Karang dynasties and the Zulu nations are considered to be among the most powerful forces in the history of the world.

However, Southern Africa remains locked within the jaws of apartheid. South Africa dominates the region to such an extent that the surrounding countries are strangled. The people of Namibia, Lesotho, Zimbabwe, and Botswana remain in an intense struggle for their very survival.

Critical Thinking Skills

Directions: Give some serious thought to the questions below. Be sure to answer in complete sentences.

1. Why can't the neighbors of the Republic of South Africa refuse to import goods from South Africa?
2. In what ways is the Republic of South Africa dependent upon its neighbors?
3. Why do you think cattle are so important to the men in Zimbabwe?
4. In what ways are the Zulus like the Native Americans in the United States?
5. What do you think the Republic of South Africa would be like if it were not governed by the descendants of Europeans?

Write It!

Directions: Imagine that you were in the Zulu army during the rule of Shaka. How would you describe your days in a letter to your best friend?

For Discussion

Directions: Discuss these questions with your class. Appoint one class member to write the ideas you discover on the board.

1. Why do you think the people of Swaziland do not eat cattle?
2. What part or parts of the United States once had laws separating blacks from whites?
3. Describe some reasons that Swaziland and Namibia are dependent upon the Republic of South Africa.
4. Explain the difference (under the system of apartheid) between the four categories of peoples in South Africa.
5. Explain why slash and burn farming is a "short-term solution to a long-term problem."

For You To Do

Directions: Many people in the United States—including senators, congressmen, college presidents, and just plain people—have condemned the system called apartheid. Write a letter to the South African embassy in Washington, D. C., and express your opinion. Include in your letter a request for an answer by someone in the embassy. Your teacher can give you the address of your school and the address of the Republic of South African Embassy in Washington.

EASTERN AFRICA

Chapter 6

F
A
C
T
S

- Tanzania has two official languages, Swahili and English.
- Mt. Kilimanjaro, at 19,340 feet, is the highest mountain in Africa.
- Somalia's official language did not have a written form until 1971.
- The people of Uganda were among the first in the world to use iron.
- Most of the islands of Comoros were formed by volcanoes.

INTRODUCTION

Eastern Africa is a land of spectacular contrasts. Along the coast, *escarpment* or sheer rock cliffs tower above the narrow *coastal plain* and the waters of the Indian Ocean. Inland, highland forests, deserts, and *grassland* form the varied *topography*. Eastern Africa is a land of breathtaking mountains, indescribable natural beauties, and countless numbers of wild animals.

Tragically, the region is also one of terrible poverty and human suffering. *Drought, famine,* and *civil war* clash with the beauty of the people and the physical setting.

Variety is the key word to remember about East Africa's *geography*. Narrow coast lowlands dominate on the east. Most of the region lies on a high *plateau* that begins at the escarpment. Magnificent mountains such as Mt. Kilimanajro (19,340 feet), Mt. Kirinyaga or Mt. Kenya (17,058 feet), and Mt. Elgon (14,176 feet) rise high above the floor of the plateau.

The Great Rift Valley is the most important feature of the geography.

EASTERN AFRICA

It is perhaps the most remarkable landform in all of Africa. This great crack in the earth seems to be a giant scar on the plateau of East Africa.

Steep sides form the edges of the rift valley and continually widen over time. The rift itself was formed thousands of years ago when a section of the East African plateau dropped down to form a narrow valley floor. Rain water has filled parts of the valley and created several great lakes. Lake Victoria, Lake Tanganyika, and Lake Malawi are three examples.

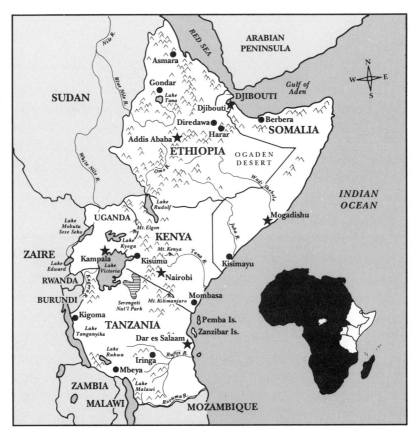

Map Study: *Which of the countries of Eastern Africa border the Indian Ocean? Among which three countries of Eastern Africa do you find Lake Victoria? In which country do you find the cities of Harar, Diredawa, and Asmara? In which part of Tanzania is the Serengeti National Park? Which East African country borders both the Indian Ocean and the Gulf of Aden?*

PART 1:
Tanzania—Land of Contrasts

Tanzania (tan zuh NEE uh) is the largest country in East Africa. It consists of two separate areas that came together in 1964—mainland Tanganyika and the island of Zanzibar, located in the Indian Ocean off the east of coast of Africa.

Mainland Tanzania is a plateau country covered by tall-tree *savannas*. The greatest landform in Tanzania is the snowcapped Mt. Kilimanjaro, located near the border with Kenya. The mountain's southern slopes are a rich agricultural region due to the rainfall and excellent soil.

The rift valley also passes through Tanzania. The famous Serengeti Plain is located here.

In addition to the geographical wonders of Tanzania, the government has set aside a huge game *reserve* called the Serengeti National Park. Tens of thousands of visitors come each year to see the huge herds of gazelles, elephants, buffaloes, and zebras. In 1987 an aerial photograph of Serengeti showed over a million animals living within the park.

Near the Serengeti Plain is the famous Olduvai (OHL duh vy) Gorge where evidence of some of the earli-

Arabs and Swahili live together in Zanzibar. Middle Eastern traders interacted with the East Africans for over a thousand years.

est human fossils known to exist have been discovered.

Tanzania was once a British colony. Through the efforts of Julius Nyerere and other nationalists, it gained its independence from Great Britain in 1961.

Over 100 *ethnic groups* contributes to Tanzania's cultural makeup. *Bantu*-speaking groups account for the majority of the country's 24 million people. The largest ethnic groups are the Sukuma, the Nyamwezi, and the Makonde.

One large nomadic group, the Masai, herds cattle, sheep, and goats along a strip of highland that extends from Kenya far into Tanzania. In this area, Masai herders burn the original *vegetation* in order to create open grasslands to graze their cattle.

Along the coast and on the islands of Zanzibar, most of the people are of Arabic background. These traditional Islamic societies maintain a *culture* that is far different from that of the plateau peoples.

Intermarriage between Arabs, who came to the area as traders and merchants, with the local Bantu people occurred widely. The merging of these two peoples created a culture that was a mix of African and Arab traditions. The new culture brought about a new language—Swahili. Today, Swahili is spoken by most people throughout all of East Africa.

Tanzania is a country of small farms. Corn, peas, beans, and wheat are the main food crops. The main cash-export crops are *sisal,* coffee,

The Masai of East Africa

The Masai live in many areas of East Africa, mostly in Kenya.

The Masai are a tall, handsome people living in most parts of Eastern Africa. They are excellent cattlemen and treat their cattle with great respect.

Curiously enough, these expert cattle herders are often undernourished and suffer from diseases of malnutrition. The Masai believe that a man is judged by how many cattle he owns. For this reason, Masai herders do not slaughter and eat the cattle. Instead, they raise cattle and sell off part of their herd from time to time.

The men of the Masai are also renowned hunters. Warriors prove their bravery by hunting and killing a lion. They do the hunting armed with only a spear and a shield.

Masai women also are well known in Africa. Masai women shave their heads and wear a great deal of jewelry made of beaded iron and copper wire.

and cotton. Zanzibar produces nearly all of the world's cloves. Copra (dried coconut meat that produces coconut oil) is also an export of Zanzibar. However, Tanzania has one very serious problem that interferes with its development. Half of the country is infested with *tsetse* flies. Few people can live in these areas.

Tanzania has many minerals, including diamonds, gold, coal, iron ore, nickel, and natural gas. Unfortunately, these deposits are neither large nor rich.

Most of Tanzania's factories make goods for local markets. Examples include food processing, oil refining, building materials, and *textiles*. Dar es Salaam (dahr es suh LAHM) is Tanzania's chief manufacturing center as well as its capital and main port. Dar es Salaam means "haven of peace" in Arabic.

Tanzanians are noted for their carvings. They are most famous for

Masks are a common form of African art.

their African masks used in religious ceremonies. Museums all over the world display masks carved by the Makonde of Tanzania.

R
E
V
I
E
W

Directions:
Answer the following questions in complete sentences.
1. Why can East Africa be called a "land of spectacular contrasts"?
2. What makes the Great Rift Valley remarkable?
3. Where does the name "Tanzania" come from?
4. Why is the Olduvai Gorge an important place?
5. What is the history of the Swahili language?

PART 2:
Uganda—An Early Civilization

Uganda (yoo GAN duh) is a story of a once great country that fell into great poverty. It is believed that civilization in East Africa may have begun in the country that is now called Uganda. Evidence of prehistoric tools is found in this area. Proof exists that animals were tamed and raised here before anywhere else in this part of the world.

Anthropologists and historians point to Uganda as the place where iron was first developed and where farming methods were first adapted. As the years passed, the peoples that lived in Uganda created great kingdoms. People from many other parts of Africa came to live in Uganda.

Today, many different ethnic groups live in this country. Bantu ethnic groups live in Southern Uganda: the Baganda, the Basoga, and the Bantoro. Other ethnic groups include the Acholi, the Lango, and the Karamajong.

The capital city of Uganda is Kampala (Kahm PAHL uh). The official language is English. However, most of the people speak a native language. Plans have been made to make Swahili the national language.

Most of Uganda lies on a high plateau. It is a nation of lakes, which cover nearly one-third of the country's area. Lakes Victoria, Albert, Kyoga, George, and Edward all fall partially or entirely within Uganda. The tall-tree savanna topography, good soil, and adequate rainfall make farming the main occupation. Coffee, tea, tobacco, cotton, and bananas are the leading cash

Anthropologists point to the area of what is now Uganda as one of the first areas of the world where the people worked with iron.

crops. The main food crops are sweet potatoes, *cassava,* corn, and beans. Cattle are another source of food.

There are copper and tin deposits to be developed. Great dams have been built on the Nile River; they can provide cheap and abundant hydroelectric power.

With all these advantages, Uganda had great potential to develop into a world-class economy. However, in 1971 a *dictator* named Idi Amin became President of Uganda. Amin became a powerful dictator. His harsh policies caused many well-educated Ugandans and Asians to leave the country.

Amin also invaded Tanzania in 1978. This act brought about a counter-invasion by the Tanzanian armies. Eventually, Amin was driven from the country. By that time, however, Uganda's economy had fallen into ruin.

Rebuilding Uganda has not been easy. Ethnic disputes between rival groups continue. However, Uganda's great agricultural *potential* still remains. A stable government can rebuild Uganda into a prosperous nation.

With all its problems, Uganda is a beautiful place. There are areas of magnificent scenery, snowcapped mountains, and thick tropical forests. Many kinds of wildlife live freely. The water regions are famous for their large number of hippopotamuses and crocodiles.

At night the river banks in this area can be dangerous. Hippos come on land to eat grass. During a nighttime feeding, hippos will usually stay close to water but may wander as far as 25 miles away. Watch out! A startled hippo can run at speeds up to 25 miles per hour.

R E V I E W

Directions:
Answer the following questions *True* or *False.*
1. It is possible that iron was first developed in Uganda.
2. Idi Amin did much to improve life in Uganda.
3. Uganda has little chance of developing a tourist industry.
4. Uganda can be called a "nation of lakes."
5. Uganda has great agricultural development potential.

PART 3:
Kenya—People and Animals

Kenya (KEN yuh) stretches from the Indian Ocean to the Great Rift Valley. It includes marshy coastal lowlands, a dry grassy central plain, and a western highland plateau. Kenya's people are unevenly distributed throughout the country. Because the northern part of Kenya suffers from a shortage of water, more than 80 percent of the people live in the south. Only 13 percent of the land is suitable for *agriculture*. In the north, Somali and Galla herders move across large areas in search of grazing lands. In the south, the Masai do the same.

The people of Kenya take great care in restoring the natural resources that they use. The Green Belt movement is a tree planting project run by Kenya's National Council of Women.

Agriculture in the highlands is increasingly concentrated on small farms. The key cash-export crops are coffee, tea, cotton, and sisal. The food crops are *sorghum*, corn, wheat, rice, sugarcane, and cassava. Kenyan farmers raise enough food to feed the people of Kenya.

Unlike many African countries, Kenya does not have many mineral resources. Therefore, its industry produces textiles, paper, plastics, soap, and processed food mainly for local use. Many factories have been built in Kenya's two major cities, the capital Nairobi (ny ROH bee) and the main port Mombasa (mahm BAHS uh). Both of these modern cities are centers of the tourist trade, which has become a major source of income for Kenya.

The plains of Kenya are densely populated by wild animal life. Thousands of *tourists* visit the country each year to shoot wild animals with camera or gun.

Much of the land in Kenya's plains has been set aside as wildlife preserves.

On and off of these preserves live un-counted numbers of *exotic* African wildlife. Elephants, cheetahs, lions, rhinoceros, hartebeests, buffaloes, gi-raffes, zebras, and many other spe-cies share this vast flat land. Croco-diles, hippos, ostriches, storks, eagles, and dozens of other types of exotic birds also live in Kenya.

Safaris hunt, track, photograph, and just watch tremendous numbers of animals that most people only see one at a time in a zoo or a circus. The business of seeing wild animals makes tourism a giant industry in Kenya.

History of Kenya

Kenya's first cities were founded by Arab and Persian traders and merchants along the coast of the Indian Ocean. The traders went inland to trade for ivory and slaves. In the 16th century, the Europeans gained control of the coastal cities. During the 19th century, the British built a railroad from Mombasa on the coast to Lake Victoria far inland. In the Kenyan highlands, the British built large productive farms. Coffee, tea, wheat, and other crops made the English rich. Along with the British settlers came workers from India and Pakistan. The local KiKuyu people

had little choice but to move to other areas or become farm workers.

In the years following World War II, Kenyans protested British colonial rule. There were peaceful demon-strations as well as outbreaks of vio-lence by a group called Mau Mau. The Mau Mau was a secret guerilla organization made up of the KiKuyu people, led by Jomo Kenyatta.

At the heart of this conflict were different attitudes toward the land. The British settlers looked on the land as personal property that cre-ated wealth and power. The KiKuyu valued land for the amount of food it could produce. In their view, the land was the property of all the people. To the KiKuyu, land could not be bought or sold.

Finally, in 1963, after a bloody revolt and civil war as Africans fought with Africans, Kenya became inde-pendent. Jomo Kenyatta became Kenya's first president.

Most Kenyans trace their *heritage* to one of the nearly 40 ethnic groups that live in Kenya today. The largest group, the KiKuyu, makes up 21 percent of the people.

Both Europeans and Arabs, with their different religious beliefs and languages, contribute to Kenya's cultural makeup. About two-thirds

SPOTLIGHT
S T O R Y

Europeans Explore Africa

European explorers searched for the source of the Nile for many years. In 1858 Richard Burton and John Speke discovered Lake Tanganyika in what is now Tanzania. Burton was certain that Lake Tanganyika was the source of the Nile, but Speke was not convinced. Speke trudged on through the jungles and discovered Lake Victoria; he became convinced that it was the source of the Nile.

In a later expedition, Speke returned to Lake Victoria. However, his travels were not without danger. At one point, his party traveled through Buganda (in what is now Southern Uganda). He was held prisoner for six months by a great king named Mutesa. Sadly, Speke died with the question of the source of the Nile unsettled.

In March of 1866, Dr. David Livingstone undertook the job of finding the source of the Nile. By this time, there were many theories as to just where the Nile began. Dr. Livingstone wandered about Africa for over five years without any communication. Many presumed that he was dead since no one had heard a word from him.

Livingstone was eventually found. A reporter from the *New York Herald*, Henry Morton Stanley, found Livingstone in a small village in November of 1871. Upon finding him, Stanley spoke the words, "Dr. Livingstone, I presume?" To which Livingstone simply responded, "Yes." These words are now part of the culture and heritage of both Great Britain and Africa.

The question about the source of the Nile, however, still went unanswered. Livingstone died in May of 1873; he had failed in his attempts to find the source of the Nile. The task then fell to Henry Morton Stanley. In 1874 Stanley set out and finally proved that Lake Victoria was indeed the source of the Nile. Upon his return in 1876, exactly 999 days after he had left, Stanley presented proof of his theories and satisfactorily disproved the theories of all the others.

Directions:
Answer the following questions in complete sentences.
1. Name four explorers who are associated with the search for the source of the Nile.
2. Identify one source of the Nile that was disproven by Henry Stanley.
3. Name three dangers that explorers faced in their search for the source of the Nile.
4. In what year did Dr. Livingstone first set out to find the source of the Nile?

Henry Stanley found David Livingstone near Lake Tanganyika in 1871.

of the people are Christian and 6 percent are *Muslims.* Swahili serves as the official language of Kenya although it is not the language of any one African tribe. Swahili includes a mixture of words from Bantu languages, from Arabic, from Portuguese, and from English.

Almost 23 million people live in Kenya today. The country is growing very fast. One reason for this growth in population is that, in Kenya, a man's success in life is measured by how many children he has. Kenyans also have large families because of necessity—it is usually a man's sons and daughters who work the farm.

Kenyans are known the world over as loyal and honest people. When a man from Kenya promises something, his word is like a sacred oath.

Calabashes and More

Kenyans are famous for their many art forms. Decorated *calabashes* or gourds are a product of the Kamba, a south Kenyan ethnic group. Calabashes are carved into containers, cooking pots, and musical instruments. In addition, Masai women are famous for their beautiful bead work.

R E V I E W

Directions:
Of the four terms listed, one does not belong. Can you spot the one term that does not belong? Write it on your paper.
1. Geography: Lake Victoria, Indian Ocean, Mt. Kenya, Atlantic Ocean
2. Peoples: KiKuyu, Masai, Galla, Mau Mau
3. Cities: Dar es Salaam, Nairobi, Mombasa, Kisumu
4. Languages: Swahili, English, French, Arabic
5. Economic Development: coffee, export crop, large mineral resources, textile production, small farm economy

PART 4:
Rwanda and Burundi—
Mountains Near the Equator

Rwanda (ruu AHN duh) and Burundi (buu ROON dee) are two very small nations in the middle of Africa. These two countries share a common climate, population, and history. Both Rwanda and Burundi are located very close to the equator. Still, they both have pleasant, cool climates because the countries are located in a mountainous region. The capital of Burundi is Bujumbura (boo jum BUUR uh) and the capital city of Rwanda is Kigali (Ki GAHL ee).

Both countries are extremely poor. Few industries and only a small amount of natural resources exist. Transportation of goods in or out of the area is very expensive because of the difficult terrain and the distance from any waterways.

In both countries, most of the people make their living as farmers. Even as farmers, the people of Burundi and Rwanda have serious problems. Both of these countries are crowded. Land is scarce. What little land there is has poor soil because of the unsuitable farming techniques used and because of *erosion*. Crops in this area include coffee, bananas, cassava, beans, and sweet potatoes. In Rwanda, many of the farmers also grow tea.

Mountainous areas in Rwanda and Burundi are good for growing tea. This plantation enjoys fertile soil and a cooler climate than might be expected so near to the equator.

The crops grown in Rwanda and Burundi depend on the *altitude.* For example, farmers raise a type of coffee called robusta on land less than 5,000 feet above sea level. Robusta is mainly used for making instant coffee. On the other hand, when the mountains rise above 5,000 feet, the coffee grown is called arabica. This arabica coffee is used for regular brewing. Both arabica and robusta coffees are grown for export.

The coffee grown high in the mountains must be sent by boat to cities in neighboring countries like Zaire and Tanzania. This long journey causes the prices to be very high. Coffee from this area of Africa is very expensive, and very little of the money goes to the farmer.

The Story of the Twa and the Watutsi

The people in these two countries form an interesting contrast. There are three ethnic groups in Rwanda and Burundi: The Twa, the Hutu and the Watutsis.

Centuries ago the Twa mingled and lived with the Hutu. The individual characteristics of the two groups have blended together over the years. Still, they have maintained many of their cultural differences.

The Watutsis invaded the area from the north. Over the years, hostility has increased. Rivalry between the groups has caused much tension between their governments. In fact, in 1961, the area separated into two countries, Rwanda and Burundi. Rwanda is mostly Hutu, and Burundi is mostly Watutsi.

The Watutsi of Rwanda and Burundi

The Watutsi see themselves as a refined, self-controlled people. They regard their traditional enemies, the Hutu, as lacking in self-control and greedy about food. For this reason, a Watutsi warrior prides himself on his ability to go for long periods of time without solid food.

A Watutsi begins his day with a bowl of curdled milk. His lunch is the same. Only after dark, with no one around him but his family, will he eat solid food. In this way, he proves himself superior to his enemies, the Hutu.

At a young age, Watutsi men are sometimes chosen to attend the king's court. There they are trained in the things that the Watutsi culture considers important. These things include bravery, readiness to take responsibility, generosity to the poor, politeness, and self-control. Additionally, they are trained in hunting skills and in the recital of poetry about the bravery of warriors in the past. The Watutsi elders also teach the young men to create such poems.

Today Rwanda is governed by a popular Hutu dictatorship. It has a prosperous small farm economy. Many successful foreign aid projects are under way. Rwanda is also popular with tourists who come to see the spectacular scenery and the mountain gorillas.

Burundi, on the other hand, is controlled by a Watutsi dictatorship. Its economy, based on cattle raising and coffee, is developing very slowly.

R
E
V
I
E
W

Directions:
Write *Yes* if the statement is true about BOTH Rwanda and Burundi. Write *No* if it is not.
1. Geography influences farming.
2. Natural resources make up a large part of their exports.
3. The different tribes get along very well.
4. Coffee is an important cash crop.
5. Modern, well-maintained roads make transportation simple.

PART 5:
Ethiopia—A Land of Ancient People

The capital city of Ethiopia (ee thee OH pee uh) is Addis Ababa (ad us SAB uh buh). The city includes a mix of modern architecture and mud houses. The official language of Ethiopia is Amharic.

Some of the oldest *fossils* of human beings are discovered in Ethiopia. Some fossils are over 4 million years old. Many scientists dig for fossils in this area in the hopes of finding clues to the beginning of mankind on the earth. In 1974 Donald Johanson, an American anthropologist working in the Afar region in Ethiopia, discovered a skeleton of a pre-human female who apparently walked upright on the African plains nearly 4 million years ago. Nicknamed Lucy, she was between 3 1/2 to 4 feet tall.

Today, Ethiopia is made up of many different ethnic groups. Often these groups do not get along with one another. One result is a poor country where thousands of people die of starvation and malnutrition each year.

Poverty is widespread among all of the groups in Ethiopia. Poor farming methods, severe drought, and war between ethnic groups have made Ethiopia one of the poorest nations in the world. Both humans and animals suffer.

The Peoples of Ethiopia

Ethiopia has many nomadic groups. These *nomads* raise cattle and

Millions of cattle have perished from the severe drought conditions that exist in Ethiopia.

depend upon rain to produce grazing lands for their herds. The nomads of Ethiopia are an ethnic group called Beja. Many Somalis also travel through this country.

Semites are people who come from Middle Eastern or Arab countries. In Ethiopia, most of the Semites are from Arabia and speak a language called Ge'ez. Semites have been a major influence upon the Ethiopian government for many years.

The Amharics have also been an important part of the government. These people are from the mountainous areas of the country.

The Galla, the Shankali, and the Falashas are other groups of considerable size in Ethiopia. Each group maintains its own heritage.

The Falashas are Jews. This group of black Hebrews claims to be descended from a lost tribe of Moses. Recently, many Falashas have left Ethiopia to live in Israel. They were aided by the Israeli Jews and airlifted to Israel.

The Land

Ethiopia lies north of Kenya. It includes very dry lowlands along its borders and a central plateau crisscrossed by mountains. When there is abundant rainfall, the fertile soil makes the plateau—home to most Ethiopians—ideal for farming. In the dry lowlands, herders and their flocks follow the rains in search of grazing lands.

Farming and Industry

Geographers believe that coffee was first used as a drink in Ethiopia.

Under the Fly in Eastern Africa

Many parts of Eastern Africa are said to be "under the fly." The fly is the tsetse fly, which causes widespread sickness and death among humans and cattle.

The tsetse fly is a medium-sized flying insect with a deep and painful bite. It carries a parasite that causes a sleeping sickness. The disease is fatal to humans if not treated promptly. In this part of Africa, doctors and medicine are very scarce.

Areas that are infested with tsetse flies are very dangerous. The insects swarm in clouds and can completely cover a cow or a human. Their sharp sting can even penetrate clothing.

Controlling the tsetse fly population is possible. Insecticides are effective against this parasite. Uganda sprayed over 3 million acres of land with insecticide and practically rid the country of the fly. However, spraying is very expensive. At the present time, many areas in Eastern Africa remain infested with tsetse flies. Signs warn, "You Are Now Entering A Tsetse Fly Area." It is a good idea to heed the warning.

When Visiting in Ethiopia

An Ethiopian home is a very private, personal place where no one is expected to visit without an invitation. When visiting someone's home for the first time, a small gift should be brought.

Visitors are expected to partake of some sort of food or drink. To refuse is considered to be quite rude. In Ethiopia, the host takes great pride in offering his guests the best meal that he can provide. It is customary to give a visitor more food than he or she could possibly eat.

But don't worry. It is also considered polite to leave some food on your plate. To your host, this act will mean that you have satisfied your appetite.

Today, coffee ranks as a major export. Farmers in Ethiopia also grow many different cereal crops. These crops include wheat, corn, sorghum, and a grain called *teff*. However, Ethiopians cannot grow nearly enough food to feed themselves. Great amounts of foreign aid are needed every year for the people to survive. Still, thousands die from starvation and malnutrition due to a severe drought and the resulting famine.

Industrial development is very limited in Ethiopia. Small factories in the capital of Addis Ababa provide goods for local markets. The area around the Eritrean city of Massawa in the north forms a second industrial region.

A Long History of Independence

Ethiopia is one of the oldest countries in the world. At one time, the influence of Ethiopia spread all the way to India in the east and to Greece in the north. It is also one of the oldest Christian nations in the world.

Many times in the past centuries, the people of this country have been invaded by outsiders. Arabs and Europeans have tried many times to conquer the people of Ethiopia. Only once were they successful; in 1935 Italy conquered and governed Ethiopia. However, the Italians were forced out seven years later in 1942.

Since the days of the powerful ancient kingdom of Axum, Ethiopia's history has often been one of quarreling small states. A ruling class—including a small noble group, the royal family, as well as the Christian (Coptic) Church—held most of the economic and political power. The majority of the people were a landless, poverty-stricken peasantry. In 1974 a combination of drought, student unrest, and years of resentment led to a revolution. The Emperor Haile Selassie, who had ruled from 1916 to 1974, was overthrown. A military-dictatorship built on a Communist model was set up. It still rules Ethiopia today.

Revolt in Eritrea

As we have learned, Ethiopia has many ethnic groups. Some of these groups have threatened to secede or break away from the country. The people of Eritrea (formerly a separate country incorporated into Ethiopia) are made up of many ethnic groups. However, they are Muslims and have little in common with the highland Christians. Since 1945 opposition to Ethiopian rule has existed. Open warfare has started again and again during the past 30 years. During the past 15 years, the rebels have been aided by Muslims in Djibouti and Somalia. These rebels are demanding independence but would probably settle for self-rule within Ethiopia.

R E V I E W

Directions:
Using complete sentences, identify each of the following.
1. Who was "Lucy"?
2. Who are the Falashas?
3. What is the tsetse fly?
4. What was the Kingdom of Axum?
5. What is the Coptic Church?

PART 6:
Djibouti and Somalia

Djibouti (juh BOOT ee) is a small country located at the entrance to the Red Sea. The area has extremely high temperatures. Although it is almost too hot to be inhabited, it has a deep harbor on the Red Sea.

Fewer than 400,000 people live in all of Djibouti. They are divided into two different ethnic groups of nomads. The Afars live in the north, and the Issas live in the south. Neither of these ethnic groups live well. Djibouti is so hot and dry that it is said that even the devil could not live there.

The capital city of Djibouti is also called Djibouti. It has two bottling plants and a harbor. No other industries or manufacturing plants exist. Most of the people in the city of Djibouti are poor.

Somalia, Land of the Nomads

Somalia (soh MAHL ee uh) is officially called the Somali Democratic Republic. It is a hot land where temperatures frequently rise above 100 degrees. It is also a dry land where very few crops can grow. Because of the conditions of Somalia, most of its people are nomads. They wander from place to place in search of grazing lands for their livestock. Livestock in Somalia almost always means cattle. However, some nomads will keep herds of goats, sheep, or camels.

The nomadic people in Somalia make up a group called the Samaal. Another group is called the Saab. The Saab live near two rivers, the

Wild animals are found in Somalia, including hyenas, lions, giraffes, hippos, and others. However, the numbers of animals found in this dry country are very small compared to those living in neighboring countries.

Juba and the Wabe Shebele. Along the banks of these rivers, they grow sugarcane, corn, or bananas.

Somalians, as a group, are highly respected as poets. Even though the Somali people have only recently adopted a written language, the children of Somalia are raised to respect the spoken word.

The Acacia Tree

A strange tree called the acacia tree grows in Somalia. Its roots grow very deep into the soil to search for water. Its canopy spreads wide to provide shade in an otherwise shadeless place. Wild animals like goats or antelope try to eat the leaves of the acacia tree. To do this, they must stand on their hind legs and be careful not to chew the sharp thorns of the tree.

Other interesting trees also grow in Somalia. The baobab tree and *aromatic* trees such as frankincense and myrrh grow in this region. These incense trees grow in the very driest parts of the country.

The combination of very dry weather with occasional wet seasons creates a perfect condition for termites. Termite columns in Somalia are a sight to behold. Often a traveler in the middle of the desert will come upon a termite mound that is 15 feet high!

REVIEW

Directions:
Change *one* word in each sentence to make the statement true.
1. Djibouti has an important deep-sea harbor on the Black Sea.
2. The people of Somalia belong mainly to the Afar and Issa nomadic peoples.
3. The Saab people are the nomads of Somalia.
4. Asmara is the capital of Somalia.
5. Much of Somalia lies along the Atlantic Ocean.

PART 7:
Indian Ocean Islands

Four island nations—Madagascar, Comoros, Seychelles, and Mauritius—lie off the east of Africa. These islands form a zone of transition between Africa and South Asia. Both regions have a great influence on these islands' cultural development. People of these islands trace their ancestry to Bantu, Asia, Arab, and European backgrounds.

Giant Tortoises

When Europeans first discovered the island of Madagascar, it was thinly populated by man. It was, however, abundant with giant tortoises. These tortoises are huge, slow moving, peaceful *vegetarians*. They may grow upwards of 500 pounds. It is likely that other islands in the area were home to the giant tortoise, but in Madagascar they lived in unbelievable numbers.

Today these tortoises are gone. They may still be found in small numbers on one or two of the smaller islands but not on Madagascar.

Giant tortoises may weigh over 500 pounds.

Madagascar

The largest of the islands is Madagascar (mad uh GAS kur). It was settled at least 2,000 years ago by people from Southeast Asia. These settlers brought with them Asian farming techniques and crops.

Arabs began to carry on trade between Madagascar and Africa's east coast. Perhaps because of this varied background, the Malagasy language has a rich literature.

The lemur, an animal related to the monkey, is found only on the island of Madagascar.

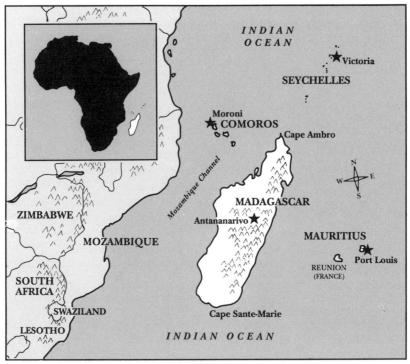

Map Study: *Off the coast of what country is Madagascar? From Comoros, in which direction would you travel to reach Madagascar? In what body of water is the island of Mauritius? Which island of Seychelles lies farthest to the east? On which East African island will you find Cape Sante-Marie and Cape Ambro?*

Along the east coast of Madagascar lies a narrow, wet coastal plain and a steep escarpment, a steep cliff capped by a flat plateau. On this escarpment can be found a mild highland climate and rich soil. West from the edge of the escarpment, the island becomes drier as it slopes down to the coast on the Mozambique Channel. This channel separates Madagascar from the African continent.

As a result of the rich soil and mild climate on the escarpment, Madagascar's farmers can raise crops of coffee, vanilla, sugar, and cloves for export. However, most farmers raise barely enough food products to survive. They raise rice, bananas, cassava, and sweet potatoes.

Comoros

The four mountainous islands of Comoros (KAHM uh rohs) are located between Madagascar and Tanzania. The official name of the nation is the Federal Islamic Republic of the Comoros.

Ships are used to export the many food products grown on the Indian Ocean islands.

Although there is a shortage of good farmland here, due to the island's mountainous topography, most Comorans work as farmers. Rice, cassava, bananas, and coconuts are grown as food products. Perfume, spices, and *copra* (dried coconut meat that produces coconut oil) are raised as cash-export crops.

In general, the Comoros are poor and very overpopulated. There are at present no minerals or natural resources found on the islands. Industry has not been much developed except for a small fishing fleet that operates along the coast. The people of the Comoros Islands must depend on foreign aid to survive.

Bananas are a large part of the economy of Comoros. Trees on these plantations will produce bananas for decades.

The people of the Comoros Islands follow the Islamic religion. The official language of the government is French. However, most of the people speak either Arabic or Swahili.

Mauritius

Mauritius (maw RISH us) is a volcanic island that lies in the Indian Ocean about 500 miles east of Madagascar. It has miles of golden beaches surrounded by colorful *coral* reefs.

Though the islands were uninhabited before their discovery in 1598, today Mauritius is densly populated. Mauritius was controlled by the Dutch, the French, and the English. Its location in the Indian Ocean between Africa and India made it a *strategic* port for supplying ships. However, the completion of the Suez Canal in 1869 caused the island to become less important.

The Europeans began the raising of sugarcane. The English language and Indian *plantation* labor were introduced after the English gained control of the island in 1810. Today the economy of Mauritius is controlled by the price of sugar on the world market.

Hindus are the largest religious group. More than one-third of the

Processing Sugarcane

Sugarcane is a plant that resembles bamboo. The stalks may grow to be three inches in diameter and up to twenty-four feet high. A good crop of sugarcane resembles a thick jungle.

After the cane is harvested and sent to the mill, it is shredded and crushed. The crushed cane is then milled or sent through heavy rollers. This pro-cess produces a liquid that is very sweet. This liquid is then processed by heating. After any impurities have been boiled away, the remaining liquid is *evaporated*. The result is a crystal that we call sugar.

people are Islamic. Mauritius has a high literacy rate and high health standards.

Seychelles

Seychelles (say SHELZ) is made up of 92 small islands, located in the Indian Ocean about 700 miles northeast of Madagascar. Because Seychelles has limited mineral resources, most people earn a living by farming. Their main products are coconuts, vanilla, and cinnamon.

Seychelles has many beautiful coral islands with miles of sandy beaches. With the bonus of year-round sunshine, an important tourist industry has been created. It provides jobs and needed cash to support the economy and the needs of the people.

In addition, a United States space tracking station on Seychelles employs many local people. This tracking station gives the United States a strategic spot from which to *monitor* spacecraft. More importantly to the people of Seychelles, it brings in American dollars needed to support the local economy. This situation is an excellent example of the interdependence between peoples who live thousands of miles apart.

R E V I E W

Directions:
Answer the following questions in complete sentences.
1. How have geographic factors influenced farming in Madagascar?
2. Why have the people of the Comoros not been able to develop a healthy economy?
3. Why has the development of the tourist industry become important in the Seychelle islands?
4. How have different ethnic groups influenced the peoples of these islands?
5. What examples of interdependence exist in relation to these islands?

EASTERN AFRICA

MAP SKILLS

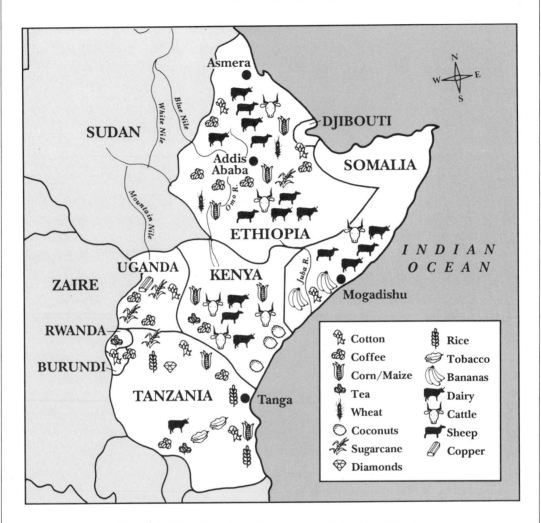

PRODUCTS OF EASTERN AFRICA

1. What are the two main products of Somalia?
2. In which country are coconuts grown?
3. What two products are grown in Burundi?
4. Which of the following are not found in Ethiopia: diamonds, cotton, coffee, or wheat?
5. What nonfood crop is grown near the city of Tanga in Tanzania?
6. What three crops are grown along the Omo River?

CHAPTER 6 REVIEW

Summary of Eastern Africa

Eastern Africa is a land of mystery, beauty, and troubles. Here lie the beginnings of the majestic Nile River, the splendor of Serengeti National Park, and the tragedy of starvation in Ethiopia. In Eastern Africa, wild animals often share the land with human beings; both frequently suffer from the harshness of drought. The drought in this part of the world has now entered its third decade. Many tens of thousands of people have been forced from their villages in search of food and water. Countless numbers have died of starvation.

Critical Thinking Skills

Directions: Give some serious thought to the questions below. Be sure to answer in complete sentences.

1. Explain why missionaries such as David Livingstone went to Africa in the first place.
2. Explain how a language and culture like Swahili might be developed.
3. Why do you think many Falashas have left Ethiopia?
4. Why are cattle so important to the Masai people?
5. How could the people of Somalia have survived for so long without a written language?

Write It!

Directions: Imagine that you are a member of the United Nations and that it is your job to see to it that the children of East Africa are properly fed. Tomorrow you are to deliver a speech to the general assembly of the UN. What will you say in your speech?

For Discussion

Directions: Discuss these questions with your class. Appoint one class member to write the ideas you discover on the board.

1. Explain why the people of Eritrea have revolted in Ethiopia.
2. What items attract tourists to a place like Kenya?
3. For what skills are the Masai famous?
4. Why do the nomads of Somalia wander from place to place?
5. What are some of the things that once made Uganda a wealthy country?

For You To Do

Directions: Go on a safari. Make a collage of some wildlife of Eastern Africa. Then, choose one species of animal and prepare a report for the class. Be sure to include these topics: what it eats, how long it lives, its size, and anything else that you think might be interesting.

NORTH AFRICA

- Eqyptians studied mathematics and astronomy as far back as 5000 B.C.
- Lybia has two capitals, Tripoli and Benghzai.
- Carpet weaving is a vital craft in many parts of Morocco.
- The once-famous fortress of Casbah is located in Algiers, Algeria.
- Over 100,000 workers were needed to build a single pyramid.

INTRODUCTION

North Africa's Arab countries include Egypt, Libya, Tunisia, Algeria, and Morocco. Located at a crossroads between Europe and Asia, North Africa has been influenced by many different cultures and traditions. Settlement is concentrated along the shores of the Mediterranean and in areas where irrigation is available.

The Sahara (suh HAR uh) is inhabited by nomadic Bedouins. The word "sahara" comes from the Arab word for great desert. Humans have lived in the Sahara Desert for thousands of years. Ancient *oasis* towns are located at springs and places where wells can reach water below dry riverbeds. The few roads crossing the Sahara follow old caravan routes from oasis to oasis.

The peoples who live in North Africa today are mostly Arabs and Berbers. Traditions are important to them, especially religion. These *Muslims* strictly follow the teachings of their holy book, called the Koran. Muslims pray in a *mosque,* a distinc-

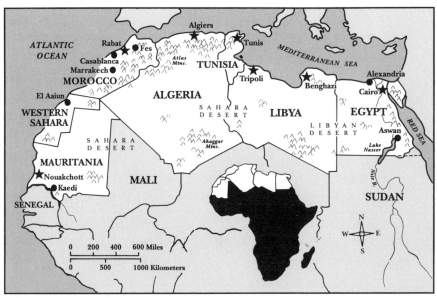

Map Study: *Which three North African countries lie within the Atlas Mountain chain? About how far from the Mediterranean Sea is Aswan? In which country do you find the cities of Marrakech, Fez, and Casablanca? What is the southernmost city in Mauritania? What North African country borders both Libya and Algeria?*

tive type of building seen very often in North African cities. The language of the people is Arabic. Important Arab civilizations have existed for thousands of years.

The Berber people are slightly more difficult to describe. Historians know that the Berbers have lived throughout North Africa for thousands of years. However, no one is sure of their origins. The Berbers maintain their own religious beliefs and their own language.

Travelers going from east to west across North Africa encounter some of the most contrasting types of land in all the world. North Africans are blessed with hundreds of miles of scenic Mediterranean and Atlantic coastlines. The majestic, *fertile* Nile River Valley and the high, snow-capped Atlas Mountains are also found in this region. In sharp contrast to these beautiful landscapes is the forbidding vastness of the Sahara Desert.

PART 1:
Egypt—An Ancient Civilization

From the Red Sea, across Egypt (EE jupt) a short distance, one can see the Nile River, the longest river in the world. Without the Nile River and an oasis here and there, very few people would live in this area because it is mainly desert. The Nile provides water, fertile crop lands, and jobs for millions of people. Cities were being built in this valley over five thousand years ago.

As far back as 4000 B.C., the Egyptians *irrigated* their farms, studied astronomy and mathematics, and made fine pottery. By 3000 B.C., these civilized people were hard at work building the great *pyramids*.

Ancient Pyramids

The great pyramids were actually tombs built for the pharaohs, the rul-ers of ancient Egypt. These huge buildings, some as long as two city blocks, were built entirely by hand. In 3000 B.C. the Egyptians did not have the machines that we have today. For that reason, as many as 100,000 people worked on the pyramids, which may have taken 20 years to build.

The sphinx of ancient Egypt was a stone figure of a lion having the head of a man. It appears that the sphinxes were used to guard the entrances to the pyramids. Except for its huge paws, the Great Sphinx seems to be carved from one piece of stone. The statue is believed to represent the god Horus and is thought to have been completed in 2700 B.C.

The Fellahin

More than half of the people in Egypt today make their living as farmers. However, only about 4 percent of the land is suitable for farming. This land is located primarily in the Nile Valley. It is farmed by *peasant* farmers called fellahin. Most of Egypt's fellahin live in villages close to their farmland.

Egyptian Cities

In contrast, Egypt has two very large cities, Alexandria and Cairo (KY roh). Alexandria serves as Egypt's major seaport and is located on the Mediterranean Sea. From this point, ships pass through the Suez Canal that joins the Mediterranean with the Red Sea.

Cairo is the capital of Egypt and the largest city in all of Africa. Over 12 million people live in this city. From Cairo, it is only a few miles to the ancient pyramids and the Great *Sphinx.* Although some parts of Cairo are thousands of years old, other parts are new. Modern Cairo looks very much the same as any large city in the United States.

R E V I E W

Directions:
Answer the following questions in complete sentences.
1. List three things that the Nile River provides to the people of Egypt.
2. Why were the pyramids built?
3. Describe some different geographical features of North Africa.
4. What is the main difference between the people of North Africa and their neighbors to the south?
5. What is the name of a Muslim house of prayer?

PART 2:
Libya and
Tunisia

To the west of Egypt is located the country of Libya (LIB ee uh). This nation is much larger than Egypt, but only about 3 million people live in the entire country. This situation occurs because most of Libya is in the Sahara.

No people can live in the Sahara unless they live near an oasis. An oasis is a spot in the desert where there is water and fertile soil. Oases depend upon seasonal rivers or deep wells for water. Some oases are found at the foot of a mountain and get their water from springs.

Because so much of Libya is desert, little farming takes place. The farmers in Libya grow barley, wheat, citrus fruits, olives, dates, and almonds. Most of the farms in Libya are found near the Mediterranean Sea. However, even near the Mediterranean rain is undependable, and very often Libya must import food.

The discovery of oil has helped to modernize Libyan cities like Tripoli and Benghazi. Both cities serve as the co-capitals of Libya. If one compares Cairo and Alexandria in Egypt to Tripoli and Benghazi in Libya, the latter two cities are smaller and newer. The skyline of Benghazi is dominated by a mix of office buildings, hotels, and mosques.

Tunisia

Northwest of Libya is Tunisia (too NEE zhuh), a small country on the Mediterranean coast. Most of Tunisia's 7 million people live near the coast.

Most farms are located in the northern part of the country. Tunisian farmers grow wheat, olives, and

Dates are the perfect crop to grow in a desert climate because they have so many uses. The fruit is edible while the leaves, trunk, and other parts can be used for building materials, for baskets, and for rope-making.

grapes. However, rain in this part of the world is scarce and unpredictable. In years of drought, the government must provide food and jobs, or many people will starve.

Many Tunisians work as fishermen. The Mediterranean Sea is like their farm. These fishermen harvest tuna, shrimp, sardines, and lobsters.

Tunis, the capital city of Tunisia, stands where Carthage used to be.

The beautiful coastline of Tunisia faces Europe, which is only 86 miles away. For over 3,000 years, Europeans have come to Tunisia to travel and to trade. Because of this exchange, Tunisia is much like a typical European country.

Hannibal's March Across the Alps

Many years ago, there was a city in Tunisia named Carthage. The Carthaginians were at war with the Romans when one of history's most famous generals, Hannibal, mounted an attack against Rome. Hannibal's army, which used elephants to carry equipment, came within 30 miles of Rome before they stopped. Many stories have been written about General Hannibal's great march across the Alps.

REVIEW

Directions:
Write *true* or *false* to describe each statement.
1. Little farming is done in Libya.
2. Libya sits atop great oil fields.
3. Oases are fed by water from the ocean.
4. Libya is smaller in size than Egypt.
5. Libya actually has two capital cities.

PART 3:
Algeria and Mauritania

Algeria (al JIR ee uh), like Tunisia, is very close to Europe. Algeria has, at different times, been ruled by Spain, Turkey, and France. Today, many Algerians still speak French.

Algeria's population clusters around the northern part of the country. Its farmers grow the typical North African crops of olives, citrus fruits, and grapes. The Saharan part of Algeria is largely unpopulated except near oases. The people there are mostly Berbers or Arabs.

Algiers (al JIRZ) is the capital city of Algeria. In Algiers, tourists often visit the Casbah, once a famous fortress, now an exciting, congested mixture of shops and housing.

Mauritania

From the western tip of Algeria, one can move south into Mauritania (mawr uh TAY nee uh). Much of this country lies in the Sahara Desert where there is nothing but endless stretches of sand. The desert continues for mile after mile, broken only by a *dune* or a few *barren* rocks.

In the south of Mauritania live the Fulani and the Tukulor. The Fulani raise mainly cattle, and the Tukulor are farmers and fishermen.

The people who live in the northern part of Mauritania are called Moors. The French call them "Maures" and named the country for them. These people are a mixture of Arabs and Berbers and *indigenous* Africans.

The Sahara seems to have been made for the Mauritanians. They are

Some Muslim women wear a jellaba and a veil that covers their face.

outstanding herdsmen and raise sheep, camels, and goats. The Mauritanians are *nomads,* which means that they move from place to place. They travel frequently so that their herds will have enough water to drink. Living in the desert for many generations has made the Moors the masters of the Sahara. They have excellent eyesight and a marvelous sense of direction.

There are no major cities in Mauritania because of the way in which the Moors live their lives. Nomads have little use for a city. Still, Mauritania has a capital city called Nouakchott (nuu AHK shaht).

The Moors depend a lot on their camels. Because of the camels' great stamina and ability to go without water for long periods, they are essential to the desert nomads of North Africa. Camels were known as the "ships of the desert."

R E V I E W

Directions:
Use a single word to complete each sentence
1. The Sahara is made of nothing but _____.
2. Mauritania is to the _____ of Algeria.
3. Mauritania is named for the people who live there called _____.
4. Nouakchott is the capital city of _____.
5. The Tukolor are farmers and _____.

PART 4:
Visiting Morocco

The last country in North Africa is called Morocco (muh RAHK oh). This nation is located at the extreme northwest corner of Africa. The high rugged Atlas Mountains cover much of Morocco. Because of their geographic location, Moroccans have long been familiar with both European and American customs.

This village is typical of those found in Morocco.

On our visit to Morocco, we will stay with the Bakkali family. They will greet us at Casablanca's modern International Airport. This is not surprising since the Moroccans practice hospitality as an art form.

Family Life

The Bakkali family is a typical Moroccan family. Malik Bakkali is a 13-year-old boy. His sister, Fatima, is two years older; and his other sister, Aisha, is eleven. Mrs. Bakkali dresses traditionally and wears a jellaba. This long, flowing cotton robe covers Mrs. Bakkali from her neck to her ankles. She also wears a veil to cover her face. Fatima has chosen to be a more modern young woman than her mother. Her dress is much like what you might see in your own neighborhood. Mr. Bakkali works in a factory in Casablanca. His clothing is also similar to what Europeans or Americans would wear.

In Morocco children between the ages of 7 and 13 must attend school. One-third of all Moroccans continue in school past the age of 13. All three children attend day school. They study the same subjects that students in the United States do, except they learn Arabic as a first language. Almost all school-aged children also learn French.

Shopping in Morocco

Before going to the Bakkali's house, we stop at the souk, or marketplace. The market in Casablanca is

The nomads of North Africa travel the Sahara Desert. They move from one water source to another, always in search of water and food for themselves and their animals.

an open market with rows and rows of stalls. In some ways, the souks are like huge malls because shoppers in the souk can buy almost anything that they need. Vendors sell fruit, fresh vegetables, eggs, candy, and even televisions! There are doctors in the markets as well as snake charmers and restaurants.

As we wander through the souk, we come to a stall full of colorful carpets that are handmade of wool and dyed in a pattern. Each family has its own unique design. Nearby are leathersmiths, goldsmiths, and many different craftsmen. Toward the outer edge of the souk, we can even buy a camel if we wish!

Mountain Villages

While in Morocco, we plan to visit a nearby mountain village. Jbila is in the foothills of the Atlas Mountains. Life is very different in Jbila than in the large city of Casablanca. The people are all farmers. There are only 20 houses in the entire village.

Village farms are very small—less than three acres. Wheat, barley, and vegetables are usually grown there. Some livestock—such as goats, chickens and perhaps a cow—can be found on a village farm. The entire family works on the farm.

People from the village travel to a nearby souk to sell their crops. That is the way they get dirhams (their money) to buy supplies. The village people might have to walk six or eight hours to get to the souk. Many village families make things themselves instead of buying them.

Evening Entertainment

When we return to Casablanca, we are going to a fantasia. The fantasia is a display of the fine horsemanship skills of the Arab and Berber riders.

As we watch, ten men in white robes and turbans race their horses toward the spectators. The men carry beautiful weapons—shiny guns and jeweled daggers. At the last second, they stop only a few feet away from where we stand. The riders fire their guns in the sky. The crowd cheers as another group of riders ready their charges.

Religion Is Very Important

The Bakkalis explained that in their religion they pray five times a day. A crier, known as a muezzin, call them to prayer from the top of the mosque's minaret or tower. Devout Muslims stop whatever they are doing, get out their prayer mats, and face Mecca. Mecca is the holy city of the Islamic or Muslim faith. It is located in Saudi Arabia.

An important observance in the Muslim religion is *Ramadan*. This holy month is the ninth month of the Islamic calendar. Each day during Ramadan, adult Muslims fast from dawn to sunset.

R
E
V
I
E
W

Directions:
Answer the following questions in complete sentences.
1. What two languages do Moroccan children learn in school?
2. What is the Arabic word for marketplace?
3. What is the unit of money used in Morocco?
4. What is the name of the crier that calls a Muslim to prayer?
5. What is the name of the Muslim holy month?

SPOTLIGHT
S T O R Y

An Evening with the Bakkalis

Before entering the Bakkali's house, we take off our shoes. Only babouches, or slippers, can be worn inside a Moroccan house. Their house is old and small. There is a kitchen, three rooms upstairs, and a storage room. Two of the upstairs rooms are bedrooms, and the third is used as a room for family gatherings. Like almost all Moroccans, the Bakkalis have a garden in the rear of the house.

Mrs. Bakkali and Fatima are preparing the evening meal. They are making the diffa, a traditional meal of welcome for visitors to a Moroccan home. As we wait for dinner to be served, Aisha settles in front of the television. In Morocco television sets are very expensive, and many families do not own one. Most television shows in Morocco are shown in Arabic or French. Because Morocco is so close to Spain, Spanish stations can also be seen on Moroccan TV.

Malik goes off to the soccer field while dinner is being prepared. He loves many sports such as basketball, volleyball, and field hockey. Swimming, track and field, gymnastics, and boxing are other popular sports in Morocco, but Malik doesn't have time to participate in each sport.

Finally, the evening meal is ready. Everyone sits around a low table. Mr. Bakkali says, "Bismillah," which means "in the name of God." Then a bowl is passed around for everyone to wash his or her hands.

Moroccans do not use forks. They eat with their right hand. It is not considered bad manners as long as your right hand is clean. The left hand is used for other tasks and is not put in the food dish.

Mrs. Bakkali begins the meal with tajine, a stew made from meat—usually chicken, pigeon, or beef. The stew is thick so that it can be eaten with the fingers. Next comes mechoui, or roast mutton. Mutton is the meat from a sheep. Then comes couscous, a boiled grain with spices or sweetening. Water is on the table, but no one takes a drink while eating.

Dessert consists of pastries and a bowl of delicious fresh oranges. Mint tea is served to the adults with dessert. The children drink orange juice or milk from crushed almonds. The Muslim religion forbids the drinking of alcohol.

After dinner Mr. Bakkali plays a flute, and Malik plays a rebab, the Moroccan fiddle. The two play classical Moroccan music called Andalusian while the women of the family clean the pots and dishes.

Stop and Review:
Directions: Write *same* if what is written is done the same way in the United States. Write *different* if it is done differently.
1. Forks are not used.
2. The large meal of the day is eaten in the evening.
3. Most television shows are in Spanish.
4. Dessert is a sweet or a piece of fruit.
5. Milk comes from crushed almonds.

CHART SKILLS

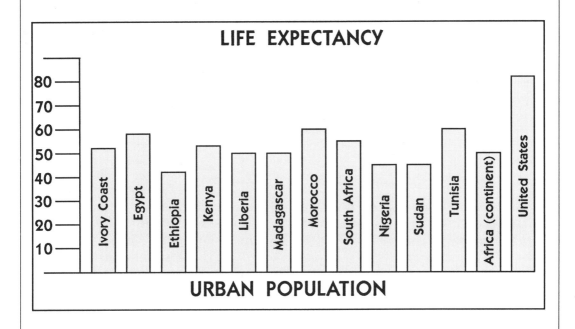

LIFE EXPECTANCY IN AFRICA

1. Which three African countries have the highest life expectancy?
2. Which African country has the lowest life expectancy?
3. Name two countries where the life expectancy is around 50 years.
4. What is the average life expectancy in all of the African countries listed?
5. What is the life expectancy in the United States?
6. What is the expected lifetime for a citizen of the Ivory Coast?

CHAPTER 7 REVIEW

Summary of North Africa

The area called North Africa is much differnet from the other regions of Africa. Their civilizations have flourished for thousands of years. The Egyptians are perhaps the oldest organized civilization in the world. North Africa has also had contact with its European neighbors for centuries. Many of the features of North Africa have been influenced by Europeans. Many of the people, too, are different. Some are lighter skinned because of their Arabic or Berber ancestry.

The North African countries can be divided into two regions. In or near the cruel Sahara Desert, nothing lives or grows. However, near the coast and along the great Nile River, cities grow and people prosper. For this reason, the North African countries are not as poor as many of their southern neighbors.

Critical Thinking Skills

Directions: Give some serious thought to the questions below. Be sure to answer in complete sentences.
1. Why are the populations of Tunisia, Algeria, and Libya clustered around the coastline?
2. How has the discovery of oil in Libya changed the way in which Libyans live?
3. Why is the varied wildlife of Equatorial and Eastern Africa not found here in North Africa?
4. How do the nomads of the desert know where to find oases?
5. What industries can be carried on in coastal cities that may not be carried on farther inland?

Write It!

Imagine being a nomad in Northern Africa. What things would you do and what would you want to have with you before you entered the desert?

For Discussion:

Directions: Discuss these questions with your class. Appoint one class member to write the ideas you discover on the board.
1. In what ways would North Africa be different without the Nile River?
2. How do the Arabs of North Africa differ from most of the ethnic groups that live in the rest of Africa?
3. Which seems to be a bigger influence on North Africa, the Nile River or the Sahara? Why?
4. Part two of this chapter stated that Tunisia is like a typical European country. What do you think this statement means?
5. How are the mountain villages of Morocco similar to the cities? How are they different?

For You To Do:

Directions: Reread the Spotlight Story in this chapter. Write a report of approximately the same length. Explain the day-to-day customs in your house. Explain to a Moroccan reader how your evening meal is eaten. Describe what members of your family are doing before and after the meal.

adobe—a building material made of sun-dried and sunbaked earth mixed with straw

Afrikaans—language of the Afrikaaners of South Africa; made up of Dutch, Bantu, and Malay words

Afrikaners—descendents of the original Dutch (Boer) settlers of South Africa

agriculture—farming; using the land to produce crops and raise livestock

altitude—height of the land above sea level

animism—the belief that spirits occupy all objects, both living and nonliving

anthropologists—people who study the science of mankind

apartheid—a system of race relations whereby the races are separated in power and status, with whites dominating blacks

aromatic—having a pleasant smell

Bantu—a group of African languages spoken generally south of a line from Cameroon to Kenya

barren—describing land with little vegetation

bauxite—a mineral ore used in making aluminum

bay—an inlet of the sea or other body of water; usually smaller than a gulf

Boers—South Africans of Dutch ancestry; the term comes from the Dutch word for farmer

bronze—a mixture of copper and another element, usually tin

cacao—the seeds of a tree from which cocoa and chocolate are made

calabash—a type of gourd

cash crop—a crop that is raised for sale and export rather than for one's own use

cassava—a plant with an edible root

caste—class or group of people

Christianity—the religion derived from Jesus Christ and based on the Bible as sacred scripture

civil war—a war among the people of a single area or country

coastal plain—a flat, sea-level area usually near an ocean

cobalt—a hard, metallic element used in making alloys

colony—a group of people living in a territory but keeping ties with the parent nation

columbite—a black mineral consisting essentially of iron and niobium

continent—a large land area of the earth

copra—dried coconut meat used to make coconut oil

coral—a skeleton deposited by sea animals

coup d'états—attempts made by the military to overthrow a government

Creole—descendents of freed slaves; also the language made by combining two or more languages

culture—the customs, beliefs, and social forms of a group of people

currency—money, both paper and coins

delta—the land at the mouth of a river

dialect—a particular form of a language

dictator—a person having complete power to rule

discrimination—treating one person or group of people better than another; prejudicial outlook, action, or treatment

dowry—money or property given by a man to or for his bride; in other cultures, it is the money or goods that a woman brings to her husband in marriage

drought—a long period of time with little or no rain

dune—a hill or ridge of sand

dynasty—a group or family that rules from one generation to the next

ebony—a very hard black wood

economics—having to do with earning a living and producing goods and services

economy—the way in which a group or nation provides for the needs and desires of its people

equator—the imaginary circle that divides the earth into two hemispheres, north and south

erosion—the wearing away of soil

escarpment—sharp, steep cliffs

ethnic group—a group of people who share a common culture and history

eucalyptus—an evergreen tree with useful wood, gums, resins, and oils

evaporated—disappeared into vapor

exceed—go over or beyond

exotic—wildly different or unusual to the beholder

export—something shipped out of one country and into another

famine—a time during which people have little or no food and many people die of hunger

fertile—describing soil or land capable of growing crops

fossils—traces of earlier life forms preserved in rock

geography—the study of the earth and people on it

goldsmith—a person who crafts gold

grassland—a large plain dominated by tall grasses

griot—a storyteller who passes down the history of a spiritual and/or ethnic group

groundnuts—an African crop; called peanuts in the United States

gulf—a part of an ocean or sea surrounded by land on three sides

haboob—a harsh wind that blows across the Sahara Desert

hardwood—wood of an angiospermous tree, one that does not produce its seeds in cones

heritage—traditions inherited or passed down from one generation to another

homelands—territories on which black South Africans are to live under the system of apartheid

GLOSSARY

illiterate—having little or no education; unable to read or write

import—buy or bring goods in from another country

indigenous—occurring naturally in an area; native

inhospitable—not friendly or receptive; providing no shelter or sustenance

intermarriage—marrying outside of one's ethnic or religious group

invincible—incapable of being conquered

irrigated—supplied water in order to grow crops

Islam—a world religion stating the belief that Allah is the only God and that Mohammed is his prophet

island—land completely surrounded by water

kraal—an enclosure for animals

lake—a body of water completely surrounded by land

landlocked—a country or place that is surrounded by land and that has no acces to a sea or ocean

mahogany—a dark, tropical hardwood, usually yellowish to reddish brown

mangrove—tropical maritime trees or shrubs with many prop roots that form dense masses

marabout—Muslim teacher

marimba—a Liberian musical instrument similar to an xylophone

marshes—areas of soft, wet land

migrate—leave one place in order to live in another

millet—a type of cereal crop

monitor—watch or observe for a special purpose

mosque—a Muslim house of prayer

Muslims—people who follow the religion of Islam

nomads—groups of people who travel from one place to another as part of their economy

oasis—a place in the desert where there is water and fertile soil

peasant—a person who has a small farm or who works on farms or plantations

piassava—a palm tree whose fibers are used to make brooms

plain—large area of flat land, sometimes with low hills

plantation—a very large farm worked by outside labor

plateau—a plain located high above sea level

polygyny—the practice of having more than one wife at a time

potential—possibility of future development and improvement

predator—an animal that hunts and kills other animals for food

preserves—(reserves) places where wild animals roam freely and are protected by law from hunters

pyramid—an ancient Egyptian construction used for burying pharaohs

rain forest—a thick tropical forest

Ramadan—the Muslim holy month

refugees—people who have left their country or region to live in another; people who flee to escape danger or persecution

republic—a nation in which people elect their leaders

reserves—(preserves) places where wild animals roam freely and are protected by law from hunters

rutile—titanium ore; a strong lightweight metal used in the manufacture of jet planes and spacecraft

safari—an expedition, usually for hunting or photographing wildlife

Sahel—an S-shaped, semidesert area in West Africa directly below the Sahara Desert; the term comes from an Arabic word meaning "shore"

sanctions—economic measures used to force a country to change its behavior or laws

savanna—a flat geographical region only slightly above sea level

Semite—a person from a Middle Eastern or Arab country

silt—dirt or sediment that is washed into and carried by rivers

sisal—a plant used in the making of rope

sorghum—a grain commonly grown in Coastal West Africa

source—place where something begins

sphinx—an ancient Egyptian construction, built to look like part man and part lion

strategic—necessary or important

subsistence—producing a minimum return and a level of bare existence

tactics—systems or planned procedures

teff—a type of grain grown in Ethiopia

terra-cotta—a baked clay used in pottery

textile—describing clothing or fabrics, such as cotton or linen

topography—the surface features of the land

tourist—a person who visits a place or country for a rest or vacation

townships—residential areas established to house black South Africans who are excluded from having homes in urban areas

tributary—a branch of a river

tropical—describing a very warm climate with much seasonal rainfall

tsetse—a type of fly that carries and spreads sleeping sickness

uranium—a radioactive element

urban—relating to a city

vegetarian—a person or animal that eats only plants

vegetation—plant life

volcanic—of or having to do with volcanoes

yams—sweet potatoes; a staple food in tropical areas

Zo—the head teacher in a bush school

INDEX

INDEX